Dr. Oetker

German Cookbook

Traditional Recipes

Dr. Oetker

German Cookbook

Traditional Recipes

Dr. Oetker Verlag

Foreword

"It tastes like home!"

The pleasure of relishing the smells and tastes of familiar regional specialities is a distinctive branch of cooking. Honest products and recipes handed down from one generation to another mean that traditions remain alive, making it possible to experience the sensual feeling of home.

The German Kitchen contains a vast range of recipes and surprising discoveries. Take a culinary journey through the regions and experience home again and again – from Fish Hamburg-style to Black Forest Schäufele, from Bavarian liver dumplings to Frisian crumble tart, from Berlin pickled pork knuckle to Rhine-style marinated beef casserole, from Frankfurt green sauce to Thuringian pork neck cutlets.

Tastes know no boundaries. For this reason, there are many recipes in German-speaking countries with cultural roots in several regions that are now valued equally in Germany, Austria, Switzerland and the Czech Republic. Familiar examples are Zurich ragout, Wiener Schnitzel, Salzburg soufflé, vanilla crescent cookies from Austria and Bohemian dumplings.

Taste your way around Germany. Bon appétit!

Sausage and cheese salad

Wurst-Käse-Salat

A fantastic outdoor side dish - perfect for your picnic hamper

Nature at peace:
St Bartholomew's church on the Königssee

4 servings

250 g/9 oz onions
250 g/9 oz Emmental cheese
350 g/12 oz pork sausage
75 g/3 oz drained gherkins (from the jar)

For the dressing:

2 tbsp white wine vinegar
2 tbsp water
1 tsp medium mustard
salt
pepper
sugar
4 tbsp cooking oil, e. g. sunflower oil
1 tbsp chopped chives

Preparation time: 35 minutes
Standing time: about 1 hour

1 Peel the onions. Cut into slices, then separate into rings. Put the onion rings in boiling water for about 2 minutes, then transfer to a sieve and leave to drain.

2 Remove the rind from the Emmental and cut into strips. Remove the skin from the sausages. Now cut the skinned sausages and gherkins into slices.

3 To make the dressing, mix together the vinegar, water, mustard, salt, pepper and sugar. Whisk in the oil. Mix together the ingredients of the salad and the dressing. Leave to stand for about 1 hour to let the flavours develop. Sprinkle the salad with chopped chives just before serving.

Tip: Sausage and cheese salad can be served as a light meal with a salted roll or pretzel, or as part of a party salad buffet. You can also prepare the salad with poultry sausage or cured smoked pork.

Kartoffelsalat mit Mayonnaise

Often served with hot dogs, cold roast meat or meatballs

4 servings
800 g/1 lb 12 oz waxy potatoes
2 onions
100 g/3 ½ oz gherkins (from the jar)
3 hard-boiled eggs

For the dressing:
6 tbsp mayonnaise
3 tbsp gherkin liquid (from the jar)
1 tbsp medium mustard
salt
freshly ground pepper

Preparation time: 45 minutes, excl. cooling time
Standing time: about 30 minutes

1 Wash the potatoes thoroughly, put in a pan filled with water, cover and boil over medium heat for about 20 minutes.

2 Drain the potatoes, quench in cold water, then drain. Peel the potatoes while they are still warm and cut into slices. Put the slices in a large bowl.

3 Peel and finely chop the onions. Cut the gherkins and shelled eggs into slices.

4 To make the dressing, stir together the mayonnaise, gherkin liquid and mustard. Mix together the ingredients with the cooled sliced potatoes and the dressing. Season with salt and pepper, then leave to stand for at least 30 minutes.

Tips: Garnish the salad with sprigs of parsley, rinsed and patted dry. Delicious with Wiener Sausages.

Süddeutscher Kartoffelsalat

Fabulous with a schnitzel at home or at a BBQ

4 servings

1 kg/2 lb 4 oz waxy potatoes
1 bay leaf

For the dressing:

2 onions
50 g/2 oz diced streaky bacon
about 100 ml/3½ fl oz (⅜ cup) cooking oil, e. g. rapeseed (canola) oil
4–5 tbsp herb dressing
125 ml/4 fl oz (½ cup) hot vegetable stock
salt
freshly ground pepper
2 tbsp chopped chives

Preparation time: 50 minutes, excl. standing time

1 Scrub the potatoes under running water, put in a pan, just cover with water and add the bay leaf. Put the lid on and bring to the boil. Cook over low heat for about 20 minutes but do not overcook; the potatoes must not be soft.

2 To make the dressing, peel and chop the onions. Fry the diced bacon in a pan with 1 tbsp oil. Now add the chopped onions, then pour in the vinegar and stock. Leave to stand for about 3 minutes, then season the dressing with salt and pepper.

3 Pour off the water from the potatoes. Drain, then peel while still hot. Cut the potatoes into slices and arrange in an ovenproof dish. Carefully fold the dressing into the sliced potatoes, then gradually add the rest of the oil. Leave the salad for a few hours for the flavours to develop.

4 Preheat the oven:
Top and bottom heat: about 150 °C/300 °F (Gas mark 2)
Fan oven: about 130 °C/250 °F (Gas mark ½)

5 Adjust the seasoning again, adding more salt, pepper and vinegar. Place the dish with the salad in the preheated oven. Leave the salad to heat up for 15–20 minutes, mixing carefully from time to time. Stir in the chives. Serve the salad warm.

Meat salad

Fleischsalat (photograph bottom right)

Easy to prepare, easy to please everyone

10 servings
600 g/1 lb 4 oz Lyoner sausage, in slices
720 g/1 lb 9 oz drained gherkins (from the jar)
50 ml/1 ½ fl oz (3 tbsp) gherkin liquid (from the jar)
1 bunch flat-leaved parsley
200 g/7 oz mayonnaise
200 g/7 oz yogurt
2 tsp medium mustard
salt
freshly ground black pepper

Preparation time: 40 minutes

1 For the meat salad, cut the finely minced pork sausage slices into halves, then into thin strips. Drain the pickled gherkins, reserving 50 ml/1 ½ fl oz (3 tbsp) of the liquid and put to one side. Cut the gherkins lengthways in slices, then cut into strips. Rinse the parsley, pat dry and remove the leaves from the stalks. Finely chop the leaves.

2 Mix together the mayonnaise, yogurt, mustard and gherkin liquid in a salad bowl and stir well. Season the dressing with salt and pepper.

3 Add the sausage and gherkin strips together with the parsley to the mixture in the salad bowl. Mix well so that all the ingredients are incorporated.

Herring salad

Heringssalat

(photograph top right)

What more could you want?

15 servings

800 g/1 lb 12 oz potatoes
7 drained Bismarck herring fillets (each 250 g/9 oz)
600 g/1 lb 4 oz cooked beetroot (beets) (vacuum packed)
5 apples, e. g. Holsteiner Cox
720 g/1 lb 9 oz drained pickled gherkins (from the jar)
5 tbsp gherkin liquid (from the jar)
5 red onions
1 bunch dill
5 tbsp mayonnaise
200 g/7 oz yogurt
2 tbsp grated horseradish
2 tsp medium mustard
1 level tsp salt
1 tbsp sugar
4 hard-boiled eggs

Preparation time: 30 minutes, excl. cooling or soaking time
Cooking time: about 20 minutes

1 Brush the potatoes clean under running water. Put in a pan, add just enough water to cover them and replace the lid. Bring to the boil and cook for about 20 minutes. Drain the potatoes, rinse in cold water, then drain again. Peel the potatoes while still warm. Leave to cool and cut into cubes. Place the herring fillets in cold water for about 30 minutes. Then remove, drain and cut into strips.

2 Cut the beetroot (beets) into cubes. Peel the apples, cut into quarters, core and cut into pieces. Drain the pickled gherkins, reserving 5 tbsp of the liquid; put to one side. Cut the gherkins into cubes. Peel the onions, cut in half and then into thin strips.

3 Mix together the cubed potatoes, strips of herring fillet, cubed beetroot, apple pieces, cubed gherkins and strips of onion in a large bowl. Rinse the dill, pat dry and pull the tops off the stems. Put a few tops to one side for the garnish. Finely chop the rest and stir into the salad in the bowl.

4 Mix together the mayonnaise, yogurt, gherkin liquid, horseradish and mustard and stir well. Season the dressing with salt, pepper and sugar, then stir into the salad. Shell the eggs, cut into quarters and fold into the salad. Garnish the herring salad with the dill tops you put aside.

Cabbage salad

Krautsalat

Very tasty. And even better with more bacon

White cabbages, as far as the eye can see

8–12 servings
1–1.5 kg/2 lb 4 oz–3 lb 4 oz white cabbage
300 g/10 oz onions
1 tsp caraway seeds
5 tbsp cooking oil, e.g. sunflower or rapeseed (canola) oil
150 g/5 oz diced bacon
5 tbsp white wine vinegar
1 tsp celery salt
1 tsp salt
½ tsp freshly ground pepper
1–2 tbsp sugar
1–2 tsp ground horseradish (from the jar)

Preparation time: 30 minutes
Standing time: about 1 hour

1 Remove the outer leaves from the white cabbage. Cut the cabbage into quarters and cut out the stalk. Cut or grate the cabbage into thin strips, rinse and leave to drain. Peel the onions and cut into fine strips. Put the cabbage and onion strips into a large bowl. Chop the caraway seeds coarsely with a few drops of oil on a chopping board (Note: the oil is to prevent the caraway seeds jumping away while being chopped).

2 Heat 1 tbsp oil in a pan. Add the diced bacon and fry until crisp. Remove the bacon from the pan and leave to drain on kitchen paper towels.

3 To make the marinade, put the rest of the oil, spices, sugar and horseradish in a pan and bring to the boil.

4 Pour the hot marinade over the salad, mix well and leave to stand for about 1 hour for the flavours to develop.

5 Just before serving, adjust the seasoning with salt, pepper, horseradish and sugar. Sprinkle the diced bacon on top.

Tip: You can serve the cabbage salad with baked meatloaf or with crisp fried bacon slices. The salad can be prepared the day before it is required. Before leaving it to stand, turn the white cabbage salad over with your hands so that the flavours are well distributed.

Variation: For a **vegetarian cabbage salad,** leave out the bacon. Instead toast 2 tbsp sunflower seeds in a pan without fat and sprinkle on the salad.

Pea soup with little sausages

Erbsensuppe mit Würstchen

Tasty and traditional:
an appealing winter warmer

4 servings
350 g/12 oz dried, unshelled peas
200 g/7 oz smoked streaky bacon
1 onion
1.5 litres/2 ¾ pints (6 cups) water, meat or vegetable stock (unsalted)
1 small stick celery
2 carrots
1 small leek
600 g/1 lb 4 oz floury potatoes
some marjoram and thyme, stems removed
salt
freshly ground black pepper
4 Wiener sausages
1 small bunch parsley

Preparation time: 20 minutes, excl. soaking time
Cooking time: 90–100 minutes

1 Rinse the peas, then soak in water for at least 12 hours. Make sure that there is enough water – about 750 ml/1 ¼ pints (3 cups) – because the peas will absorb a lot of it. Then pour the peas into a colander to drain.

2 Cut up the bacon into small cubes. Peel the onion, cut in half and chop up finely. In a large pan on medium heat, add the cubes of bacon and render down, then add the diced onion and fry until transparent.

3 Add the water, meat or vegetable stock and the peas. Cover and cook the ingredients for about 1 hour.

4 In the meantime, clean the celery, carrots and leek and cut into small pieces. Peel the potatoes, rinse, drain thoroughly and cut into cubes. Put in a pan, add just enough water to cover all the ingredients and put to one side.

5 After cooking the pea mixture for an hour, add the potatoes together with the cooking water. Add the marjoram and thyme. Season the soup with salt and pepper. Then cover and cook for another 30–40 minutes over low to medium heat.

6 Cut the small sausages into slices. Rinse the parsley and pat dry; then pull the leaves off the stems and chop finely.

7 Add the sliced sausages to the soup and heat up in the soup. Season the pea soup again with salt and pepper and sprinkle with parsley before serving.

Tips: Only season the peas with salt when they are cooked. Otherwise they will need longer to cook.
The amount of water or stock indicated in the recipe only applies to the shortest cooking time. If necessary add more water or stock later.
Instead of parsley you can also use chopped chives to garnish the soup.
The pea soup is also very delicious when warmed up the following day.
It is excellent for freezing.

Lentil stew with pork sausages

Linseneintopf mit Mettwürstchen

Perfect for keeping out winter chills

4 servings

1 bunch soup vegetables (carrots, celery, leeks)
250 g/9 oz dried lentils
375 g/13 oz waxy potatoes
2 onions
2 tbsp cooking oil, e. g. sunflower or rapeseed (canola) oil
1.5 litres/2 ¾ pints (6 cups) meat or vegetable stock
4 pork sausages (smoked, each about 90 g/3 oz)
white wine vinegar
salt
freshly ground black pepper
1 pinch sugar
2 tbsp coarsely chopped parsley

Preparation time: 25 minutes
Cooking time: about 25 minutes

A typical half-timbered house in North Rhine-Westphalia

1 Clean and peel the carrots. Peel the celery. Wash the celery and carrots and drain. Clean the leeks, cut in half lengthways, wash carefully and drain. Chop up all the vegetables you have prepared for the soup.

2 Put the lentils in a sieve and rinse under cold water. Peel the potatoes, rinse, drain and cut into cubes. Peel the onions, cut in half and then into slices.

3 Heat the oil in a pan and as soon as it hot, add the prepared vegetables and potatoes and fry. Then add the meat or vegetable stock, bring to the boil, cover and cook for about 20 minutes over medium heat.

4 Cut the sausages into slices and add to the pot shortly before the end of the cooking to warm up.

5 Season the stew with vinegar, salt, pepper and a little sugar and sprinkle with parsley before serving.

Tip: You can also add 1 bay leaf to the stew and remove it before serving.

Potato soup

Kartoffelsuppe

This hearty, traditional soup is full of earthy goodness

4–6 servings
500 g/18 oz floury potatoes
100 g/3 ½ oz celery
1 onion
100 g/3 ½ oz leeks
40 g/1 ½ oz (3 tbsp) butter
800 ml/28 fl oz (3 ¼ cups) meat or vegetable stock
150 g/5 oz crème fraîche
a little chopped marjoram
a little grated nutmeg
salt
ground white pepper

Preparation time: 15 minutes
Cooking time: 20–30 minutes

1 Peel the potatoes and celery, rinse, drain and cut into cubes. Peel the onion, cut in half and then into cubes. Clean the leeks, make an incision lengthways and wash thoroughly; then drain and cut the leeks into the thinnest strips possible.

2 Melt the butter in a pan. Add the diced onion and fry until transparent. Add the diced potatoes and celery and strips of leeks. Fry briefly and add the stock. Bring to the boil, cover and cook over medium to low heat for 20–30 minutes.

3 Then puree the soup with a stick blender, reheat briefly, then stir in the crème fraîche.

4 Season the potatoes with the spices listed.

Tips: For **potato soup with Westphalian caviar,** sprinkle 2 tsp poppy seeds into the soup. The soup is also delicious if you add thin strips of ham, smoked salmon or croutons.
To make the soup even lighter, replace the crème fraîche with 100 g/3 ½ oz whipped cream.

Three-meat stew

Pichelsteiner

For the real Bavarian Forest feeling: original, traditional and substantial

Living tradition. The Pichelsteinerfest has been celebrated in Regen, Bavaria, since 1874.

4 servings

500 g/18 oz mixed meat from the shoulder or neck (lamb, pork, beef)
2 onions
30 g/1 oz (2 tbsp) clarified butter or margarine or
3 tbsp cooking oil
salt
freshly ground pepper
chopped marjoram
chopped lovage
500 ml/17 fl oz (2 cups) meat or vegetable stock
250 g/9 oz carrots
375g/13 oz waxy potatoes
350 g/12 oz leeks
300 g/10 oz white cabbage
2 tbsp chopped parsley

Preparation time: 20 minutes
Cooking time: about 1 hour

1 Pat the meat dry with a kitchen paper towel and cut into cubes of about 2 cm/¾ in. Peel the onions and cut into slices.

2 Heat the clarified butter, margarine or oil in a pan. Add the cubes of meat and stir to fry them lightly all over. Then add the onion slices and fry them briefly with the meat.

3 Season the meat with salt, pepper, marjoram and lovage. Add the stock, bring to the boil, cover and cook over medium heat for about 40 minutes.

4 Meanwhile clean the carrots, peel, rinse, then leave to drain. Peel the potatoes, rinse and leave to drain. Cut both vegetables into cubes. Prepare the leeks, cut them in half lengthways, wash thoroughly, leave to drain and cut into slices. Remove any limp, withered outer leaves from the cabbage. Cut the cabbage into quarters and cut out the core. Cut the cabbage into thin strips. rinse, and leave to drain.

5 When the meat is cooked, add the vegetables and potatoes you have just prepared and bring to the boil again.

6 Season with salt and pepper, cover and cook for about another 20 minutes.

7 Season the stew again with more herbs and sprinkle with parsley before serving.

Tip: Add 1 parsnip. To clean the parsnip, peel, rinse, drain and cut into cubes. Add the parsnip with the other prepared vegetables in step 5.

4 servings
500 g/18 oz Kasseler smoked pork (without bones)
2 onions
1 tbsp cooking oil, e. g. sunflower oil
salt
freshly ground black pepper
about 500 ml/17 fl oz (2 cups) vegetable or meat stock
750 g/1 lb 10 oz swedes (rutabaga)
500 g/18 oz waxy potatoes
1 tbsp chopped parsley

Preparation time: 30 minutes
Cooking time: about 50 minutes

1 Dry the smoked pork with kitchen paper towel and cut into small cubes. Peel the onions and cut into cubes.

2 Heat the oil in a pan, add the cubed pork and fry until light brown, stirring continuously. Add the diced onion and fry briefly. Season with salt and pepper. Now add half the stock, bring to the boil, cover and cook over medium heat for about 30 minutes.

3 Meanwhile peel the swedes and potatoes, rinse and cut into sticks. Add the swede and potato sticks together with the rest of the stock to the pan with the meat. Season with salt and pepper, cover and cook for another 20 minutes.

4 Adjust the seasoning again and sprinkle with the chopped parsley.

Tips: You can also add some medium mustard. And if you like you can also add dried, crushed marjoram or garnish the hotpot just before serving with 1–2 rinsed, drained, thinly-sliced spring onions.
The swede hotpot is ideal for freezing.
Instead of Kasseler (smoked pork), you can also use shoulder of lamb.

Variation: for a **swede hotpot with lentils,** add 100 g/3 ½ oz lentils and cook according to the instructions on the packet. Use about 1 litre/1 ¾ pints (4 cups) vegetable stock to cook the lentils.

Swede hotpot

Steckrübeneintopf

A great pleasure – spoonful by spoonful

Green beans hotpot

Grüne-Bohnen-Eintopf

Germany is known for its delicious stews. This one brings fresh colour to your table

4 servings

500 g/18 oz braising beef (without bones, lean)
40 g/1 ½ oz (3 tbsp) margarine or 4 tbsp cooking oil, e. g. olive oil
1 onion
salt
freshly ground black pepper
750 ml/1 ¼ pints (3 cups) vegetable stock
800 g/1 lb 12 oz green beans
500 g/18 oz potatoes
2 sprigs savory

Preparation time: 25 minutes
Cooking time: about 45 minutes

1 Pat the beef dry with kitchen paper towel and cut into 2 cm/¾ in cubes.

2 Heat the margarine or oil in a pan, then add the cubed meat and brown lightly while stirring.

3 Peel the onion and cut into dice. Add the diced onion to the pan and continue frying briefly.

4 Season the meat with salt and pepper, add half the stock, cover and braise for about 20 minutes.

5 Top and tail the green beans. If necessary remove any stringy fibres, wash, drain and cut or break into small pieces. Peel the potatoes, rinse, drain and cut into cubes.

6 Rinse the savory and pat dry. Add the savory, green beans, cubed potatoes and the rest of the stock to the pan. Bring to the boil and cook for another 25 minutes until done.

7 Season the stew with salt and pepper. Remove the savory before serving.

Tips: You can further enhance the stew by adding 250 g/9 oz of peeled, de-seeded and cubed tomatoes or a carrot, previously peeled, rinsed and cut into small dice.

Creamed asparagus soup

Spargelcremesuppe

Asparagus – the true harbinger of summer

4 servings
500 g/18 oz white asparagus
1 tsp salt
1 tsp sugar
60 g/2 oz (4 tbsp) butter
1 litre/1 ¾ pints (4 cups) water
about 300 ml/10 fl oz (1 ¼ cups) milk
30 g/1 oz (¼ cup) plain (all purpose) flour
½ bunch parsley
ground white pepper
grated nutmeg
2 egg yolks (medium)
3 tbsp whipping cream

Preparation time: 45 minutes
Cooking time: about 35–37 minutes

1 Peel the asparagus from top to bottom. Make sure that all the stringy outside is removed while being very careful not to damage the heads. Cut off the ends (the woody parts should be completely removed). Put the peelings and ends to one side. Cut the asparagus into pieces 3 cm/1 ¼ in long.

2 Put the asparagus ends and peelings in a pan. Add salt, sugar and 20 g/¾ oz (1 ½ tbsp) butter, pour in the water, bring to the boil, cover and cook over medium heat for about 15 minutes.

3 Pour the asparagus ends and peelings through a colander, collecting the cooking liquid and bring it to the boil again. Add the pieces of asparagus, bring to the boil, cover and cook for 10-12 minutes until al dente.

4 Put the pieces of asparagus in a colander to drain and again keep the cooking liquid. Top up with milk to make 1 litre/1 ¾ pints (4 cups).

5 Melt the rest of the butter in a pan. Add the flour and stir until the mixture is pale yellow. Pour in the asparagus-milk liquid little by little, stirring vigorously with a whisk, making sure there are no lumps.

6 Bring the soup to the boil and simmer without a lid for about 10 minutes, stirring occasionally.

7 Rinse the parsley, pat dry and pull the leaves off the stems. Chop up two-thirds of the parsley.

8 Season the soup with salt, sugar, pepper and nutmeg. Mix together the cream and egg yolks and stir 4 tbsp of the soup into the cream-egg yolk mixture.

9 Now add the resulting mixture back to the soup, but do not let the soup boil again. Add the drained pieces of asparagus and warm up briefly. Garnish the soup with parsley before serving.

Tips: If you like, cut up 50 g/2 oz cooked ham into thin strips and warm up in the soup with the pieces of asparagus. You can also make the soup with green asparagus. In this case only peel the bottom third of the stem. Cook the green asparagus pieces for about 8 minutes.

The asparagus harvest is carried out by hand. Each spear is picked separately.

Bayerische Leberknödel

Bavarian liver dumplings

Enjoy them with a pretzel!

4 servings
3–4 day-old bread rolls (180–200 g/7 oz)
100 ml/3 ½ fl oz (⅜ cup) milk
salt
freshly ground black pepper
125 g/4 ½ oz calf`s liver
2 shallots
2 sprigs marjoram
2 sprigs parsley
2 tbsp butter
2 egg yolks (medium)
some breadcrumbs (optional)

Preparation time: 30 minutes, excl. rising time
Cooking time: about 10 minutes

The Frauenkirche is the symbol of Munich

1 Cut the rolls into small cubes and put in a bowl. Season the milk with salt and pepper, then bring briefly to the boil. Pour the hot milk over the cubed rolls and stir well with a wooden spoon. Leave the bread and milk mixture to stand for at least 30 minutes, stirring occasionally.

2 Pat the calf's liver dry with kitchen paper towel and if necessary remove any skin, sinews and veins. Cut up the liver into small cubes.

3 Peel the shallots and chop finely. Rinse the marjoram and parsley, pat dry and pull the leaves off the stems.

4 Melt the butter in a small pan. Add the chopped shallots and fry until golden. Now add the fried shallots together with the chopped marjoram, parsley and egg yolks to the bread and milk mixture and mix well. Puree the cubed liver until smooth and also add to the bread and milk mixture.

5 Season the liver mixture with salt and pepper and shape into 8 meatballs (dumplings) with moistened hands. The mixture must be thick enough to enable you to make dumplings from it. If the mixture is too thick, you can add some more warm milk. If the mixture is too liquid, add some breadcrumbs to thicken it.

6 Plunge the liver dumplings in salted boiling water and cook for about 10 minutes until done (the water should only bubble very, very lightly).

7 Remove the liver dumplings from the water with a skimming ladle and serve.

Tips: For a **liver dumpling-soup,** make small quenelles from the liver mixture using two teaspoons. Cook them in boiling meat stock, add thin strips of vegetables and you have a delicious soup. Other possibilities are to serve the liver dumplings with a herb sauce or on a bed of vegetables. You can replace the fresh marjoram with 1 tsp dried marjoram and the fresh parsley with 1 tsp dried parsley.

Pickled pork knuckle with sauerkraut

Eisbein mit Sauerkraut

One of Berlin's most famous dishes – a huge portion of local atmosphere

4 servings
1.5 kg/3 ¼ lb pickled pork knuckle (4 pieces, if necessary order from the butcher in advance)
about 1.75 litres/3 pints (7 cups) water

For the sauerkraut:
750 g/1 lb 10 oz fresh sauerkraut
1 onion
1 bay leaf
3 cloves
5 juniper berries
250 ml/8 fl oz (1 cup) meat stock
1 floury potato
salt
freshly ground black pepper
a little sugar

Preparation time: 20 minutes
Cooking time: 1 ½–2 hours

A corner pub in Berlin: a welcoming casual meeting place for locals and tourists alike.

1 Rinse the pickled pork knuckle under cold running water. Put the water and pork in a pan, bring to the boil, cover and cook over low to medium heat for 1 ½–2 hours.

2 Meanwhile loosen the sauerkraut with a fork and peel the onion. Put the sauerkraut, onion, bay leaf, cloves, juniper berries and stock to a pan and bring to the boil. Cover and cook the sauerkraut for about 30 minutes. If necessary add a little stock from the pork cooking liquid.

3 Peel the potatoes, rinse and drain. Grate the potatoes, add the sauerkraut and briefly bring to the boil again so that it becomes creamy. Season the sauerkraut with salt, pepper and sugar.

4 Remove the pickled knuckle of pork from the pan and serve with the sauerkraut.

Accompaniment: Boiled potatoes or potato puree.

Tip: Sauerkraut preserved in a jar or canned is usually pre-cooked. In that case all you need to do is heat it up and season it.

8 servings

For the marinade:

2 carrots
3 parsnips
1 stick celery
1 onion
1 pinch salt
2 bay leaves
½ tsp peppercorns
½ tsp mustard seeds
3 cloves
1 clove garlic
1 sprig thyme
5 allspice
250 ml/8 fl oz (1 cup) herb or wine vinegar
1 litre/1 ¾ pints (4 cups) beef stock
1 litre/1 ¾ pints (4 cups) red wine

2 kg/4 ½ lb beef without bones (from the leg)
2 tbsp lard
salt
freshly ground black pepper
2 tbsp sugar syrup
2 tbsp cranberries (from the jar)

For the sauce:

2 tbsp crème fraîche
a little cornflour (cornstarch)
100 g/3 ½ oz (¾ cup) raisins
4 tbsp slivered almonds

Preparation time: 50 minutes, excl. cooling or marinating time
Cooking time: about 2 hours

1 For the marinade, clean the carrots, parsley roots and celery. Peel, rinse and drain them, then cut into pieces. Peel and coarsely chop the onion. Transfer the prepared vegetables into a pan. Add the remaining ingredients for the marinade, bring to the boil and leave to cool. Put the marinade in a large bowl or soufflé dish.

2 Wipe the beef dry with kitchen paper towel and add to the marinade. Cover and marinate the beef for at least 24 hours in the refrigerator. In the case of a large piece of beef, allow more time for marinating so that the beef has time to absorb the marinade.

3 Preheat the oven:
Top/bottom heat: about 200 °C/400 °F (Gas mark 6).
Fan oven: about 180 °C/350 °F.

4 Remove the beef from the marinade and pat dry with kitchen paper towel. Pour the marinade through a sieve into a pan.

5 Melt the lard in a roasting pan. Add the beef and brown briskly on all sides, then season with salt and pepper. Add the well-drained vegetables (from the marinade) and fry briefly.

6 Add the sugar syrup and cranberries and stir well. Now add the marinade liquid. Cover the roasting pan and put in the preheated oven. Cook the sauerbraten for about 2 hours until ready.

7 Remove the beef from the roasting pan and keep in a warm place.

8 Strain the sauce and stir in the crème fraîche. If you like, thicken the sauce with cornflour (cornstarch) and cook briefly. Stir in the raisins and almonds. Season the sauce with salt and pepper. Add the beef to the sauce.

9 Before serving, cut the Rheinische Sauerbraten into slices and arrange the slices on a dish. Then either pour the sauce on top or serve the sauce with it.

Accompaniment: Potato dumplings and red cabbage.

Rhine-style marinated beef casserole

Rheinischer Sauerbraten with alcohol

Traditionally prepared with raisins in the Rhineland

Rinderrouladen

Beef roulade

A classic German Sunday dish

4 servings
4 spring onions
1 carrot
4 slices beef (each 180–200 g/7 oz , from the leg)
4 tsp medium mustard
salt
freshly ground black pepper
8 slices bacon (about 160 g/5 ½ oz)
3 tbsp cooking oil, e.g. rapeseed oil
250 ml meat stock

Optional:
20 g/¾ oz (3 tbsp) plain (all purpose) flour
3 tbsp cold water
1 spring onion

Also:
wooden toothpicks or roulade needles

Preparation time: about 30 minutes
Cooking time: about 1 ½ hours

1 Clean the spring onions, rinse, wipe dry and cut in half. Peel the carrots, rinse, drain and slice.

2 Pat the beef dry. Put the beef slices side by side, coat with mustard and sprinkle with salt and pepper.

3 Place 2 slices of bacon and 2 spring onion halves on each slice of beef. Roll up from the narrow side. Secure the roulades with toothpicks or roulade needles.

4 Heat the cooking oil in a large, flat pan. Add the roulades and brown briskly on all sides. Add the carrots and the rest of the spring onions and fry briefly with the rest.

5 Add the stock and braise the roulades for about 1 ½ hours. Turn the roulades from time to time and add more stock or water if necessary.

6 Arrange the cooked roulades on a preheated dish. Remove the toothpicks and place the roulades in a warm place.

7 Add water to the cooking juices to make up to 500 ml/ 17 fl oz (2 cups), bring to the boil and puree with a stick blender.

8 If you like, mix together flour and cold water and stir this mixture into the boiling sauce. Continue cooking the sauce for about 5 more minutes, season with salt and pepper. Clean the spring onions, rinse, pat dry, cut into thin slices and stir into the sauce.

Tip: You can also add a little mustard to add a kick to the sauce.

Accompaniment: Serve with **red cabbage.** To make red cabbage: remove the outer leaves of a 1 kg/2 ¼ lb red cabbage. Cut into four. Cut out the stalk. Cut the red cabbage into very thin strips or grate, rinse and drain. Peel 375 g/13 oz sharp apples, cut into quarters and cut our the core. Cut the apples into small pieces. Peel 2 onions and cut into cubes. Heat 5 tbsp cooking oil or 50 g/2 oz (3 tbsp) goose fat in a pan. Add the diced onions and fry briefly, stirring all the time. Now add the red cabbage strips and pieces of apple and continue frying. Add 1 bay leaf, 3 cloves, 5 juniper berries , 5 grains allspice, salt, pepper, a little sugar, 2 sticks cinnamon, 2 tbsp red wine vinegar, 3 tbsp redcurrant jelly and 125 ml/4 fl oz (½ cup) water. Cover and braise the red cabbage over low heat, stirring occasion-ally. Season with salt and sugar.

Black Forest Schäufele

Schwarzwälder Schäufele with alcohol

The tenderest meat – a salted, smoked delight

4 servings
1 litre/1 ¾ pints (4 cups) water
1 onion
500 ml/17 fl oz (2 cups) white wine
1 tsp salt
3 cloves
1 bay leaf
4 juniper berries
5 peppercorns
1–2 tsp dried thyme
750 g/1 lb 10 oz salted, lightly smoked pork shoulder

Preparation time: 15 minutes
Cooking time: about 1 ½ hours

1 Bring the water to the boil in a pan. Peel the onion and add to the pan together with the wine, salt, cloves, bay leaf, juniper berries, peppercorns and thyme. Bring to the boil again.

2 Wipe the shoulder of pork dry with kitchen paper towel. Add the meat to the pan, bring to the boil again and skim if necessary. Cover and cook the meat over low heat for about 1 ½ hours until done.

3 Remove the meat from the pan, cut into slices and serve.

Accompaniment: Cubed potatoes sprinkled with fresh herbs and creamy sauerkraut. To make the sauerkraut, cook the sauerkraut as usual, then stir in some béchamel sauce.

The most striking feature of the Black Forest costume is the ladies' hat, the Bollenhut. Only genuine with 11 visible pompoms – red for unmarried girls and black for married women

Erfurt – one of the oldest cities in Germany

Thuringian pork neck cutlets

Thüringer Rostbrätel with alcohol

Timing is important: marinate at length, cook quickly

6 pieces
1 kg/2 ¼ lb pork neck without bones
2–3 onions
1 clove garlic
200 g/7 oz medium mustard
500 ml/17 fl oz (2 cups) beer, e. g. Pils or black lager
salt, freshly ground black pepper
marjoram, stems removed
caraway seeds

Preparation time: 15 minutes, excl. marinating time
Grilling (broiling) time: 5–10 minutes

1 Dry the pork neck with kitchen paper towel and cut into 6 pieces of similar size.

2 Peel the onions and garlic. Press the garlic through a garlic press. Cut the onions into rings. Mix together the onion rings, garlic and mustard and stir in 200 ml/7 fl oz (¾ cup) of the beer. Season the marinade with salt, pepper, marjoram and caraway.

3 Arrange the slices of meat in a bowl and pour the marinade on top. Cover and leave in the refrigerator for 1–2 days, turning the slices once.

4 Allow the slices of meat to drain briefly and cook under a grill (broiler) preheated to medium heat for 5–10 minutes, depending on the thickness of the slices.

5 Pour on a little of the marinade and the remaining beer each time you turn the slices over (this will prevent the meat from drying out and the steam will further enhance the flavour of the meat).

Tip: Fry the meat in the pan. To do this, heat 2 tbsp of cooking oil in a large pan. Add the slices of meat in portions and fry with mushrooms for 5–10 minutes, turning once.

Kasseler mit Sauerkraut with alcohol

Smoked pork with sauerkraut

Always a firm favourite – once you've tried it, you'll want it again

6 servings

For the meat:

800 g–1 kg/1 lb 12 oz/2 lb 4 oz smoked pork neck (without bones)
1 onion
1 bunch soup vegetables (carrots, celery, leeks)
1 small bay leaf
125 ml/4 fl oz (½ cup) hot water
some dark gravy thickener (optional)
salt
freshly ground black pepper

For the sauerkraut:

2 apples
1 bay leaf
4 juniper berries
1 tsp caraway seeds
1 tsp peppercorns
500 g/18 oz sauerkraut
125 ml/4 fl oz (½ cup) white wine
125 ml/4 fl oz (½ cup) water
1 medium potato
a little sugar

Preparation time: 30 minutes
Roasting time: 50 minutes
Cooking time: 30 minutes

1 Wipe the pork dry with kitchen paper towel and make crisscross incisions in the layer of fat.

2 Preheat the oven:
Top/bottom heat: about 200 °C/400 °F (Gas mark 6)
Fan oven: 180 °C/350 °F

3 Peel the onion. Clean the soup vegetables, rinse, drain and cut all the vegetables and the onion into small cubes.

4 Place the meat with the layer of fat facing upward in a roasting pan rinsed in water. Add the cubed vegetables and onion together with a bay leaf. Put the roasting pan in the preheated oven (bottom third). Cook the meat for about 50 minutes.

5 When the cooking juices begin to brown, add a little hot water. Replace the evaporated liquid gradually by adding hot water. Baste the meat now and again with the cooking juices.

6 Meanwhile make the sauerkraut. Peel the apple, cut into quarters, core each quarter and grate. Put the herbs in a paper coffee filter and tie up. Put the sauerkraut with the grated apple, bag of herbs, wine and water in a pan. Cover and simmer for about 30 minutes.

7 Peel the potatoes, rinse and grate finely. Stir into the sauerkraut halfway through the cooking time, to make it creamy. Remove the bag of herbs and season the sauerkraut with salt, pepper and a little sugar.

8 When the meat is cooked, cover and leave to rest for about 10 minutes so that the meat juices become distributed.

9 Make the sauce by adding some water to the pan, then scrape the cooking residues and stir well. Push the sauce and vegetables through a sieve, return to the heat and bring to the boil again. If you like, thicken the sauce with gravy thickener and bring briefly to the boil again. Slice the meat and arrange the slices on a warmed dish. Season the sauce with salt and pepper and serve with the meat and sauerkraut.

Accompaniment: Potato puree, mustard and/or fresh farmhouse bread.

The Oktoberfest, or "Wiesn" for short, is the largest festival in the world

Knuckle of pork

Schweinshaxen

They'll bring that Oktoberfest atmosphere to your kitchen

4 servings
4 pork knuckles (each about 500 g/18 oz)
salt
freshly ground black pepper
some hot water
3 medium onions

Preparation time: 20 minutes
Cooking time: about 80 minutes

1 Preheat the oven:
Top/bottom heat: about 200 °C/400 °F (Gas mark 6)
Fan oven: about 180 °C/350 °F (Gas mark 4)

2 Rinse the meat under cold running water, wipe dry, then rub salt and pepper into the meat. Place the meat in a roasting pan, previously rinsed in water.

3 Put the roasting pan on the shelf in the preheated oven (bottom third). Cook the meat for about 80 minutes. As soon as the cooking juices begin to brown, add a little hot water.

Baste the meat now and again with the cooking juices, replacing the evaporated liquid gradually as necessary.

4 About 30 minutes before the end of the cooking time, peel the onions, cut into quarters and add to the roasting pan with the meat. Continue cooking the meat until it is done.

5 Then remove the meat from the roasting pan, cover and place in a warm place. Make the sauce by adding some water to the pan, then scrape the cooking residues and stir well. Push the sauce and vegetables through a sieve, return to the heat and bring briefly the boil again. Season with the condiments, then add the sauce to the meat.

Accompaniment: Creamed peas or sauerkraut with potato puree or simply fresh farmhouse bread and cold beer.

Tip: You can add a little heat to the sauce by stirring in some mustard.

Variations: You can also use veal instead of pork, following the same recipe. The cooking time is then 2½–3 hours.

Boiled beef with horseradish sauce

Tafelspitz mit Meerrettichsauce

Time spent preparing this Viennese delicacy will be well rewarded

4 servings

1–1.5 litres/1 ¾ –2 ¾ pints (4 ½–7 cups) water
1 kg/2 lb 4 oz beef topside (round)
salt
1 bay leaf
1 tbsp peppercorns
2 large onions
150 g/5 oz carrots
150 g/5 oz celery sticks
200 g/7 oz leeks

For the horseradish sauce:

30 g/1 oz (2 tbsp) butter or margarine
25 g/1 oz (4 tbsp) plain (all purpose) flour
375 ml/12 fl oz (1 ½ cups) beef stock
125 g/4 ½ oz whipping cream
20 g/¾ oz freshly ground horseradish
salt
some sugar
about 1 tsp lemon juice
1 tbsp chopped parsley

Preparation time: 20 minutes
Cooking time: about 2 hours 20 minutes

1 Bring water to the boil in a large pan. Pat the meat dry with kitchen paper towels and add to the boiling water together with the salt, bay leaf and peppercorns. Cover and simmer the meat for about 2 hours over low to medium heat.

2 Meanwhile peel and chop the onions. Prepare the carrots and celery, peel, wash, leave to drain and cut into slices. Prepare the leeks, cut them in half lengthways, wash thoroughly and leave to drain; cut into pieces about 2 cm/¾ in long.

3 When the meat has cooked, add the vegetables you have just prepared, cover and cook for a further 20 minutes.

4 Cover the meat and leave to rest for about 10 minutes before slicing to let the meat juices settle. Strain the stock with the vegetables through a sieve, reserve the stock and measure 375 ml/12 fl oz (1 ½ cups) of it for the sauce. Cover the vegetables and keep in a warm place.

5 While the meat is resting, melt the butter or margarine for the horseradish sauce in a small pan. Add the flour and stir until the mixture has become pale yellow. Add the reserved 375 ml/12 fl oz (1 ½ cups) boiled beef stock and the cream. Beat the sauce briskly with a whisk, making sure that there are no lumps. Bring the sauce to the boil while stirring all the time, then simmer over low heat without a lid for about 5 minutes, stirring occasionally.

6 Stir in the horseradish. Season the sauce with salt, sugar and lemon juice. Cut the meat into slices and arrange them on a warmed dish; then pour some hot stock over them. Sprinkle the boiled beef with parsley and serve with the vegetables and the sauce.

Serve with: roast potatoes, green salad or carrots.

Tips: You can also make the sauce with horseradish from the jar instead of fresh horseradish.
Boiled beef can also be frozen in its broth.

Variations: To make **herb sauce,** mix together 3 tbsp mayonnaise, 150 g/5 oz crème fraîche, 150 g/5 oz yoghurt, 100 g/3½ oz whipping cream and ½ tsp medium mustard. Stir 3 tbsp chopped mixed herbs into the sauce. Season with salt and pepper.

To make **cold horseradish sauce,** mix together 150 g/5 oz crème fraîche with 2 tbsp horseradish from the jar and season with a little lemon juice, salt, pepper and sugar.

To make a **chives sauce,** finely dice 1 peeled shallot and 1 prepared carrot (about 100 g/3½ oz). Blanch the carrots for about 1 minute in salted boiling water, then plunge in ice-cold water. Mix together 150 g/5 oz crème fraîche with 4 tbsp olive oil and 1 tbsp white wine vinegar. Rinse 1 bunch of chives, pat dry and chop into rings. Stir the vegetables and chives into the sauce. Season with salt and pepper and serve with the boiled beef.

Cured pork ribs with sauerkraut

Schweinerippchen mit Kraut

A culinary highlight as a main course or as a snack

2 servings

1 litre/1 ¾ pints (4 cups) water
500 g/18 oz cured pork ribs
1 onion
2 tbsp rapeseed oil
500 g/18 oz fresh sauerkraut
1 apple
3 juniper berries
1 bay leaf
about 200 ml/7 fl oz (¾ cup) meat stock

Preparation time: 40 minutes

1 Bring water to the boil in a pan. Place the pork chops in the pan and bring to the boil again. Cover and cook the chops for about 30 minutes.

2 Peel and finely chop the onion. Heat the oil in a pan, add the chopped onions and fry.

3 Add the sauerkraut and fry for about 5 minutes, stirring occasionally.

4 Peel the apple, cut into quarters, core and cut into cubes, then stir into the sauerkraut together with the juniper berries and the bay leaf.

5 Pour in the stock and stir well. Cover and bring to the boil, then cook for about 20 minutes.

6 Cut the chops into portion-size pieces and arrange on the sauerkraut before serving.

Accompaniment: Potato puree.

Tips: Serve with a little mustard. Remove the juniper berries and bay leaf from the sauerkraut before serving.

Pork schnitzel with creamy mushroom sauce

Jägerschnitzel

An evergreen favourite, and mushrooms were never so delicious!

Porcini – pretty as a picture!

4 servings

1 onion
250 g/9 oz mushrooms
4 pork escalopes, each about 200 g/7 oz
salt
freshly ground black pepper
sweet paprika powder
40 g/1 ¼ oz (⅓ cup) plain (all purpose) flour
50 g/2 oz (3 tbsp) margarine
or 5 tbsp cooking oil, e. g. sunflower oil
150 g/5 oz crème fraîche
1 tbsp chopped parsley

Preparation time: 35 minutes

1 Peel and finely chop the onion. Clean the mushrooms, if necessary rinsing them briefly and patting dry. Cut the mushrooms into slices.

2 Pat the pork escalopes with kitchen paper towel, season with salt, pepper and paprika. Coat the escalopes with flour, then shake off excess flour.

3 Heat the margarine or oil in a pan. Add the escalopes and cook over medium heat for 10–12 minutes (depending on the thickness) on both sides, turning occasionally. Take the escalopes out of the pan and keep in a warm place.

4 Fry the chopped onion in the remaining fat in the pan, stirring all the time. Add the sliced mushrooms and continue frying. Now stir in the crème fraîche. Season the sauce with salt and pepper and simmer over low heat without a lid for 2–3 minutes. Then stir in the parsley. Serve the sauce with the escalopes.

Accompaniment: Chips or fried potatoes with a green salad.

Tip: You can use other kinds of mushrooms such as chanterelles, button mushrooms and/or porcini.

Wiener Schnitzel

Wiener Schnitzel

Authentically Viennese and as famous as the waltz and the Vienna Philharmonic

The famous ferris wheel in Vienna's Prater is visible from far away

4 servings

For the escalopes:

4 veal escalopes (each 120 g/4 oz, from the upper leg)
or 8 small cutlets (each 60 g/2 oz)
salt
freshly ground black pepper
2 eggs
2 tbsp whipping cream
50 g/2 oz (scant ½ cup) plain (all purpose) flour
150 g/5 oz (¾ cup) breadcrumbs
200 g/7 oz (1 cup) clarified butter or margarine
4 slices organic lemon (untreated, unwaxed)

Preparation time: about 45 minutes

1 Rinse the escalopes under cold running water and wipe dry. Pound them until they are slightly thinner, then season with salt and pepper.

2 Whisk together the eggs and cream. Coat the escalopes lightly in flour, shake off excess flour, then dip into the egg-cream mixture and coat in breadcrumbs. Press gently to make them adhere.

3 In a large pan, heat the clarified butter or margarine until very hot; do this in portions if the escalopes will not fit all at once. Add the escalopes let them "swim" in the fat, frying on both sides for 2–3 minutes depending on the thickness. Then remove the escalopes and leave to drain on kitchen paper towel.

4 Garnish the escalopes with slices of lemon.

Accompaniment: Fried potatoes or potato salad and green salad.

Tip: Instead of veal, you can use pork escalopes (about 150 g/5 oz each). In this case fry for 3–4 minutes.

Goulash

Gulasch

Typically Hungarian and as hot as you like

4 servings
500 g/18 oz onions
500 g/18 oz lean beef, e.g. topside (round)
30 g/1 oz (2 tbsp) margarine or 3 tbsp cooking oil, e.g. sunflower oil
salt
freshly ground pepper
sweet paprika
2 slightly heaped tbsp tomato purée
about 250 ml/8 fl oz (1 cup) hot water
1–2 drops Tabasco sauce

Preparation time: 15 minutes
Braising time: 1 ¼–1 ½ hours

1 Peel the onions and cut in half, then cut the onion halves into slices. Pat the meat dry with kitchen paper towels and cut into cubes of about 3 cm/1 ¼ in.

2 Heat margarine or oil in a pan. Add the meat cubes in two instalments and brown briskly on all sides. Add the rest of the margarine or oil and the sliced onions and fry together.

3 Season with salt, pepper and paprika, then stir in the tomato purée. Add hot water to cover. Put a lid on the pan and cook for 1 ¼ to 1 ½ hours over medium heat. If there appears to be too little liquid at any time, add a little water.

4 Season the goulash with salt, pepper, ground paprika and Tabasco sauce.

Tips: Use lean pork instead of beef (braise for about 45 minutes).
Add a sophisticated touch to the goulash by replacing half the water with red wine.
Goulash is suitable for freezing.

Serve with: noodles or rice and cucumber salad.

Zurich ragout

Züricher Geschnetzeltes with alcohol

A dish as iconic as Swiss chocolate and the Alps.

4 servings
2 medium onions
500 g/18 oz veal (from the leg)
2 tbsp plain (all purpose) flour
3 tbsp butter or margarine
125 ml/4 fl oz (½ cup) white wine
250 g/9 oz whipping cream
salt
freshly ground black pepper
1 pinch sugar

Preparation time: 30 minutes

Lake Zurich offers peace and relaxation away from the city centre

1 Peel and finely chop the onion. Pat the meat dry with kitchen paper towel. Cut the meat into paper-thin slices and sprinkle with flour.

2 Heat 1 tbsp of the butter or margarine in a non-stick pan. Add a quarter of the chopped onions and half the meat and fry for about 2 minutes, stirring occasionally (the meat must not brown!), then remove from the pan. Put the meat in a bowl and keep in a warm place, covered with a plate.

3 Heat another tablespoon butter or margarine. Add the rest of the meat and another quarter of the chopped mushrooms and cook in the same way.

4 Melt the rest of the butter or margarine, add the rest of the chopped onions, fry for about 3 minutes and stir the wine. Now add the cream and meat, season with salt, pepper and sugar. Heat the ragout for about 5 minutes and serve immediately.

Tip: You can also add an extra 200 g/7 oz of cleaned mushrooms, cut into slices, to the last portion of chopped onions. Then continue as indicated in the recipe.

Accompaniment: Serve with **rösti.** To make the rösti, brush clean 500 g/18 oz firm potatoes under cold running water, add just enough water to cover the potatoes, put a lid on the pan, bring to the boil and cook for about 20 minutes. Then pour away the water, plunge in cold water and drain. Peel the potatoes while still warm, cover and leave in the refrigerator for at least 4 hours, or even better, overnight. Grate the potatoes coarsely, season with salt and pepper. Heat 6 tbsp cooking oil in a pan (diameter 24 cm/9½ in). Now add the grated potatoes to the pan, press flat slightly, then cook over low heat on both sides for about 10 minutes until brown and crisp, turning once. Cut the rösti into 4 pieces if you like.

Meatballs with carrots

Frikadellen mit Möhrengemüse

The perfect beef, egg and bread roll mix, great at home or for picnics

4 servings

For the meatballs:

1 day-old bread roll
2 onions
2 tbsp cooking oil, e.g. sunflower oil
600 g/1 lb 4 oz minced (ground) meat (half beef, half pork)
1 egg (medium)
2 tsp hot mustard
1 tbsp finely chopped parsley
1 pinch de-stemmed marjoram
grated zest of ½ organic lemon (untreated, unwaxed)
salt
freshly ground black pepper

For the carrot dish:

750 g/1 lb 10 oz baby carrots
50 g/2 oz (3 tbsp) butter
100 ml/3½ fl oz (⅜ cup) water
1–2 tbsp chopped parsley
40 g/1½ oz (3 tbsp) clarified butter, margarine or 5 tbsp cooking oil, e.g. sunflower oil

Preparation time: 35 minutes

1 For the meatballs, soak the roll in cold water. Peel and finely chop the onions. Heat the oil in a pan, add the chopped onions and fry for 2–3 minutes until transparent, stirring all the time. Remove the onions from the pan and drain on kitchen paper towel.

2 Squeeze the roll to remove as much water as possible, then mix together with the minced meat, chopped onion, egg, mustard, herbs and grated lemon zest. Season the meat mixture with salt and pepper. With wet hands, make 8 meatballs from the meat mixture.

3 To make the carrot dish, clean the carrots, peel, rinse and leave to drain. Then cut into halves or quarters depending on the size. Melt the butter in a pan, add the carrots and fry for 2–3 minutes. Add water and just a little salt, cover and cook the carrots for about 10 minutes, stirring occasionally. Season the carrots with salt and pepper and stir in the parsley.

4 Heat the clarified butter, margarine or oil in the pan and fry the meatballs on both sides over medium heat for about 10–15 minutes until brown and done, turning them over occasionally.

Accompaniment: Potato puree.

Tip: You can make the meatballs even crispier by coating them in breadcrumbs before frying them. If there are any left over, they are also delicious cold, or you can cut them into slices and have them in a sandwich. Knead some small diced bell peppers into the meat mixture.

Bratwurst

The German fast-food tradition at its best

4 servings
4 parboiled or fresh bratwurst sausages
(each about 120 g/4 oz)
2 tbsp cooking oil, e. g. sunflower oil

Preparation time: 15 minutes

1 Dry the sausages with kitchen paper towel. Fresh sausages should be pricked several times all over with a fork.

2 Heat the oil in a pan. Add the sausages and fry without lid until brown over medium heat for about 10 minutes on both sides, stirring occasionally.

Accompaniment: Potato puree, carrots and kohlrabi as vegetables, ketchup and mustard.

A German classic for more than 60 years: the curried sausage

Variation 1: For **Berliner curried sausage,** stir 150 ml/5 fl oz (⅝ cup) water in a pan together with 1 tsp curry powder, ½ tsp each hot and sweet paprika, 1 tsp sugar, 1 pinch each allspice, cumin and chili powder. Bring everything to the boil and simmer for 3–4 minutes. Remove the pan from the heat. Stir together 2 tbsp Worcestershire sauce and 250 g/9 oz ketchup and bring briefly to the boil, stirring all the time. Keep the sauce in a warm place but do let it cook anymore. Pat dry 4 bockwurst sausages (thick Frankfurters, with the skin, cooked and smoked, each about 100 g/3½ oz) with kitchen paper towel and make 5–6 incisions to prevent them bursting open. Heat some cooking oil (e. g. sunflower oil) in a deep pan. (There should be enough oil in the pan that about a quarter of the thickness of the sausages is "swimming" in the oil.) Fry the sausages on each side over medium heat until crisp and golden. Cut the sausages into bite-size pieces, put in a bowl, pour the still-warm curry sauce on top and sprinkle with a little curry powder. Serve with a roll, braised onion rings or raw, spicy chopped onion.

Tips: In many parts of Berlin the curried sausage is not cut into bite-size pieces but cut in half. Then the curry sauce is poured over the top together with a generous sprinkling of curry powder.
You can also use 4 wollwurst sausages (white sausage without skin, about 100 g/3½ oz each) instead of bockwurst. Fry them as described above until a nut brown crust has formed all round. The sausage will remain crisp if you pour the sauce next to it.

Variation 2: For **Ruhr-style curried sausage,** put 120 ml/4 fl oz (½ cup) water in a pan. Add 1 tsp sugar, 2 tsp curry powder and ½ tsp cayenne pepper, stir well and bring to the boil. Remove the pan from the heat, stir in 200 g/7 oz ketchup, continue stirring without stopping and bring briefly to the boil. Pat dry 4 thin sausages (with the skin, not smoked, about 100 g/3½ oz each). Heat 2 tbsp cooking oil in a pan. Fry the sausages on both sides over medium heat until brown, turning occasionally. Then cut into bite-sized pieces, put in bowl, pour the still-warm curry sauce on top, sprinkle with curry powder with a slice of white bread.

Saddle of venison Baden-style

Badischer Rehrücken with alcohol

How about some deer, my dear

4 servings
1 saddle of venison on the bone (about 1.6 kg/3 ½ lb)
salt
freshly ground black pepper
75 g/3 oz streaky bacon slices
1 onion
50 g/2 oz celery
100 g/3 ½ oz carrots
5 juniper berries
125 ml/4 fl oz (½ cup) dry red wine
100 ml/3 ½ fl oz (⅜ cup) vegetable or veal stock
2–3 pears, e.g. Williams Christ
200 ml/7 fl oz (¾ cup) sweet white wine
juice of 1 lemon
250 ml/8 fl oz (1 cup) dry red wine
100 g/3 ½ oz crème fraîche
180 g/6 ½ oz cranberry compote
dark sauce thickener (optional)
sprigs of rosemary to garnish (optional)

Preparation time: 30 minutes
Cooking time: 35–50 minutes

1 Preheat the oven:
Top/bottom heat: about 200 °C/400 °F (Gas mark 6)
Fan oven: about 180 °C/350 °F

2 Pat the saddle of venison dry with kitchen paper towel and if necessary, remove the skin. Rub salt and pepper into the meat. Place the saddle in a roasting pan, previously rinsed in water, and cover with the slices of bacon.

3 Peel and finely chop the onion. Clean, peel and rinse the celery and carrots, then leave to drain and chop up. Add the vegetables to roasting pan and put in the preheated oven on the middle shelf. Cook for 35–50 minutes. As soon as the cooking juices begin to brown, add the juniper berries, red wine and vegetable or veal stock.

4 Meanwhile wash the pears under hot water, cut in half and core (easiest with a melon-baller). Put the pear halves in a pan together with the white wine and lemon juice, then bring to the boil. Cover and braise over medium heat for about 10 minutes. Remove the pears from the liquid and leave to cool.

5 Remove the venison from the roasting pan, cover and leave to rest for about 10 minutes so that the meat juices become distributed. Deglaze the cooking residues with red wine, push the vegetables through a sieve, bring to the boil and stir in the cream. Add 2 tbsp cranberry compote, bring to the boil again and allow to bubble for 3–5 minutes. You can stir some of the meat juices from the resting meat into the sauce. If you prefer the sauce thicker, add gravy thickener or reduce the sauce until it acquires a syrupy consistency; then season again with the condiments.

6 Remove the slices of bacon. Remove the meat from the bone, cut into slices and rearrange back on the bone. Place the saddle of venison on a warmed dish and sprinkle with rosemary to taste.

7 Fill the pear halves with the rest of the cranberry compote and arrange round the saddle of venison. Serve the sauce separately.

Accompaniment: Spätzle and red cabbage or Brussels sprouts.

Tips: If you want to prepare the venison without alcohol, you can replace the red wine with redcurrant, cranberry or cherry juice. To carve the venison (cutting it into portions): place the saddle on a board with the bone downward. With a sharp knife make an incision along the middle bone, then cut along the lower bone to remove the meat. Then cut the meat into slices or pieces.

Stuffed goose

Gefüllte Gans

A goose is a treat, and not just for Christmas

8 servings
1 oven-ready goose (4–4.5 kg/9–10 lb)
salt
freshly ground pepper
dried chopped marjoram or sage

For the stuffing:
50 g/2 oz streaky bacon
2 onions
20 g/¾ oz (½ tbsp) butter or margarine
about 8 day-old bread rolls
300 ml/10 fl oz (1 ¼ cups) milk
4 eggs (medium)
2 tbsp chopped parsley
2 apples
about 500 ml/17 fl oz (2 cups) hot water
1 bunch soup vegetables (celery, carrots, leeks)
about 100 ml/3 ½ fl oz (⅜ cup) cold water
10 g/⅓ oz (4 tsp) plain (all purpose) flour

Also:
cooking string or wooden skewers

Preparation time: 45 minutes, excl. cooling time
Roasting time: about 4 ½ hours

1 Rinse the goose under running cold water and pat dry. Rub the goose inside and out with salt, pepper and marjoram.

2 To make the stuffing, cut the bacon into cubes. Peel and finely chop the onion. Melt the butter or margarine in a pan. Add the diced bacon and fry until crisp. Then add the chopped onions, sweat until transparent and put to one side.

3 Preheat the oven.
Top and bottom heat: about 200 °C/400 °F (Gas mark 6)
Fan oven: about 180 °C/350 °F

4 Cut the rolls into small cubes and put in a bowl. Heat the milk in a pan, pour over the diced roll and mix well together. Now stir in the diced bacon and onion mixture and leave to cool a little.

5 Stir in the eggs and parsley and season the mixture with salt. Peel the apple, cut in half, remove the core, grate and stir into the mixture. Stuff the goose with the mixture. Close the cavity by sewing the skin with cooking string or by securing it with wooden skewers. Rub the outside of the goose all over with salt, pepper and marjoram or sage.

6 Place a roasting pan on a shelf in the bottom third of the preheated oven. Pour in 125 ml/4 fl oz (½ cup) hot water. Place the goose on a grid, breast side down, then put this grid above the roasting pan in the preheated oven. Cook the goose for about 1 ½ hours. Prick the goose several times in the underside of the wings and legs so that the fat can drain out easily. Skim off the fat which has collected.

7 As soon as the cooking residues begin to brown, add hot water until the water is about 1 cm/⅜ in deep in the roasting pan. Baste the goose regularly with the cooking juices. Replace the evaporated liquid with more hot water when necessary.

8 Meanwhile clean, rinse and drain the vegetables, then cut into small pieces.

9 After about about 1 ½ hours, turn the goose over. Add the vegetables to the roasting pan and continue cooking for about another 3 hours.

10 Stir ½ tsp salt into 50 ml/1 ½ fl oz (3 tbsp) cold water. About 10 minutes before the end of the cooking time brush this all over the goose and increase the oven temperature

by about 20 °C/35 °F so that the skin becomes beautifully crisp. Remove the goose from the oven, cover and leave to rest for 5–10 minutes to let the juices settle.

11 Scrape the cooking residues from the bottom of the roasting pan, adding a little water. Pour through a sieve, add water to make 600 ml/21 fl oz (2½ cups) and transfer into a saucepan. Bring to the boil.

12 Stir the flour into 50 ml/1½ fl oz (3 tbsp) water until smooth and beat into the hot liquid, using a whisk. Make sure no lumps are formed. Bring the sauce to the boil and simmer gently without a lid for about 5 minutes over low heat, stirring occasionally. Season the sauce with salt, pepper and marjoram.

13 Carve the goose into individual servings, arrange on a warmed serving dish and serve with the sauce.

Accompaniment: Potato dumplings and Brussels sprouts or red cabbage.

Tip: For a larger goose, increase the cooking time by about 30 minutes per 1 kg/2¼ lb.

Labskaus

8th Avenue in Brooklyn, New York, is nicknamed Lapskaus Boulevard!

4 servings
600 g/1 lb 4 oz sliced salted beef
6 large onions
1 bay leaf
3 cloves
500 ml/17 fl oz (2 cups) water
75 g/2 ½ oz (⅓ cup) butter or margarine
1 kg/2 ¼ lb cooked potatoes, still warm
6 tbsp pickled gherkin liquid (from the jar)
375 ml/12 fl oz (1 ½ cups) meat stock (from the cooked beef)
salt
grated nutmeg

Preparation time: 45 minutes
Cooking time: about 2 hours

Hamburg's church of St Michaelis, nicknamed "Michel", seen from the port

1 Pat the beef dry with kitchen paper towel. Peel 1 onion and make an incision for the bay leaf. Insert the bay leaf and the stalk ends of the cloves in the onion.

2 Put water in a pan, cover and bring to the boil. Add the beef, cover again, bring to the boil and cook for about 1 ½ hours. Drain the beef and cooking liquid in a colander, putting 375 ml/12 fl oz (1 ½ cups) aside. Remove the clove-studded onion.

3 Peel the 5 remaining onions. Coarsely chop the meat and onions. Put both through a meat mincer (grinder). Melt the butter or margarine in a pan. Add the meat-onion mixture and fry for about 5 minutes, stirring all the time.

4 Peel the potatoes and push through a potato press while still warm. Add the mixture together with gherkin liquid and meat stock to the meat and onion mixture and mix well to incorporate all the ingredients. Bring all to the boil and cook thoroughly, stirring all the time.

5 Season with salt and nutmeg.

Accompaniment: Roll mops, fried egg, gherkins and/or beetroot (beets).

Tips: If you do not have a meat mincer (grinder), you can chop up the meat and onion very finely.
Instead of pickled meat you can also use corned beef.
You can also add 2 rinsed salted herring fillets when you process the meat and onions.

Fish Hamburg-style

Hamburger Pfannfisch

Ready, steady, cook!

4 servings
500 g/18 oz large potatoes of equal size
150g/5 oz (⅔ cup) butter
500 g/18 oz mixed fish fillets, e.g. haddock, plaice and cod (skinned and boned)
4 shallots
2 tsp medium mustard
250 g/9 oz young Savoy cabbage
salt
freshly ground black pepper

For the mustard sauce:
2 shallots
1 tbsp sunflower oil
100 ml/3½ fl oz (⅜ cup) fish or vegetable stock
100 g/3½ oz whipping cream
2 tbsp medium mustard
80 g/3 oz (generous ⅓ cup) chilled butter
1 pinch chili powder

Preparation time: 50 minutes, excl. cooling time
Cooking time: about 15 minutes

1 Peel the potatoes, rinse and wipe dry. Cut the potatoes into slices about 5 mm/3⁄16 in thick.

2 Melt 50 g/2 oz (3 tbsp) of the butter in a pan. Add the potato slices and fry them, turning them over several times.

3 Preheat the oven:
Top/bottom heat: about 200 °C/400 °F (Gas mark 6)
Fan oven: about 180 °C/350 °F (Gas mark 4)

4 Rinse the fish under cold running water, pat dry and cut into slices about 2 cm/¾ in thick.

5 Peel the shallots, first cut into slices, then separate into rings. Melt 50 g/2 oz (3 tbsp) of the remaining butter in a second pan. Add the shallot rings and fry until transparent, leave to cool, then stir in the mustard.

6 Clean the Savoy cabbage, wash, drain and cut into thin strips. Blanch the cabbage strips in boiling water for about 2 minutes, plunge in ice-cold water and leave to drain in a colander.

7 In a greased springform mould (diameter 24 cm/9½ in), arrange one-third of the fried potato slices in a circular pattern on the base and sprinkle with salt and pepper. Arrange half the cabbage strips on top, then half the fish slices; sprinkle with salt and pepper. Spread the shallot-mustard mixture on top.

8 Repeat this process and finish with the rest of the fried potato slices. Sprinkle with salt and pepper. Melt the rest of the butter, leave to cool and pour over the potatoes. Put the springform mould in the preheated oven. Bake for about 15 minutes.

9 Put the springform mould on a wire rack and leave to cool.

10 To make the mustard sauce, peel and finely chop the shallots. Heat the oil in a pan, add the chopped shallots and fry until transparent. Add the stock and cream, stir in the mustard and heat up the sauce. Cut the butter into thick cubes and stir into the sauce. Season the sauce with salt, pepper and chili powder. Remove the pan from the heat and keep the sauce warm.

11 Remove the side of the springform mould. Arrange the cooked fish, cabbage and potato on a warmed dish and cut into slices like a cake. Serve with the mustard sauce.

Matjesfilets nach Hausfrauen-Art

Reminiscent of harbours, fishing boats and the sea

4 servings
8 herring fillets (about 600 g/1 lb 4 oz)
250 ml/8 fl oz (1 cup) water
salt
3 onions
400 g/14 oz sharp apples, e.g. Cox's Orange
drained pickled gherkins (from the jar)
200 g/7 oz whipping cream
150 g/5 oz crème fraîche or sour cream
3 tbsp lemon juice
freshly ground black pepper
sugar

Preparation time: about 30 minutes, excl. standing time

Visitors from all over Europe come to Emden's annual herring festival

1 Rinse the fillets under cold running water and pat dry. If necessary remove any bones you may find and cut the fillets into 2 cm/¾ in pieces.

2 Bring water to the boil in a pan. Add ¼ tsp salt. Peel the onions and cut into slices. Blanch the onion slices briefly in the boiling water, then leave to drain.

3 Peel the apples, cut into quarters and remove the core. Cut the apples and gherkins into slices.

4 Stir together the cream, crème fraîche and lemon juice, season with salt, pepper and sugar. Now stir in the onion, apple and gherkin slices. Add the pieces of herring filet to the sauce, cover with clingfilm (plastic wrap) and place in the refrigerator for about 12 hours to enable the sauce to develop its flavours fully.

Accompaniment: Potatoes in their skins, fried onion rings and green beans.
In Westphalia it is eaten with fried potatoes (page 83) and drained cocktail gherkins and/or drained beetroot (beets) (both from jars).

Tip: This dish is particularly good with a very cold beer. Garnish the herring fillets with finely-chopped dill, rinsed and patted dry.

Fresh trout from the lake
to the table

Forelle blau with alcohol

Poached or fried?
You don't have to decide – try both!

4 servings
4 prepared trout (each about 200 g/7 oz)
1 onion
375 ml/12 fl oz (1 ½ cups) white wine
750 ml/1 ¼ pints (3 cups) salted water
5 tbsp vinegar
1 bay leaf
5 peppercorns
4–5 juniper berries
3–4 sprigs flat-leaved parsley
1–2 organic lemons (untreated, unwaxed)
1–2 tbsp olive oil

Preparation time: 30 minutes

1 Rinse the trout inside and out under cold running water. When doing so, make sure you do not damage the outer mucous layer (otherwise the trout will not become blue). Pat the fish dry. Peel the onion and cut into quarters.

2 Bring the white wine and salted water to the boil in a large pan together with the onion quarters, vinegar, bay leaf, peppercorns and juniper berries. Allow the mixture to boil for 2–3 minutes.

3 Add the fish to the boiling mixture and bring everything to the boil again. Cover and cook over medium heat for 15–20 minutes. As soon as the back fins can be pulled out easily, the trout are ready.

4 Meanwhile rinse the parsley, pat dry and pull the leaves from the stems. Wash the lemon or lemons under hot water, wipe dry and cut into thin slices.

5 Remove the cooked trout from the liquid, drain and arrange on plates. Sprinkle the trout with a little olive oil and garnish with the parsley leaves and lemon slices.

Accompaniment: While the trout are cooking you will still have time to prepare a **chives yogurt** as a garnish or side dish. To make chive yogurt, rinse 1 bunch of chives, pat dry and cut up finely. Stir the chopped chives into 300 g/10 oz yogurt. Season with freshly ground pepper and salt.
A classic side dish consists of boiled potatoes (750 g/1 lb 10 oz, weight unpeeled) tossed in butter with 1 tsp salt.

Variation: For **trout meunière,** rinse the trout as described above and season. Then coat in 40 g/1 ¼ oz (⅓ cup) plain (all purpose) flour and shake off the excess. Heat 3 tbsp sunflower oil in a pan. Add the trout and fry on both sides over medium heat. Now add 40 g/1 ½ oz (3 tbsp) butter and allow to melt. Fry the trout for about 10 minutes, turning them several times. Garnish with organic lemon slices, previously rinsed and patted dry.
For **trout with almonds,** add 50–75 g/2–3 oz (½–¾ cup) slivered almonds to the pan, allow to brown and pour over the trouts before serving.

4 servings
2 carp (each about 1.5 kg/3 ¼ lb, filleted by the fishmonger and cut in half along the spine)
salt
freshly ground black pepper

For baking:
100 g/3 ½ oz (generous ¾ cup) plain (all purpose) flour
50 g/2 oz (½ cup) semolina flour

cooking fat

Preparation time: 25 minutes, excl. standing time
Frying time: 10–15 minutes

Carp breeding ponds in Franconia's Aischgrund fish-farming area

1 Rinse the carp halves under cold running water and pat dry. Sprinkle with salt and pepper and leave to stand for about 30 minutes.

2 Mix together the flour and semolina.

3 Put a sufficient amount of cooking fat in a large, deep pan and heat to about 175 °C/350 °F so that when you hold a wooden spoon in the fat, bubbles form round it.

4 Coat the carp halves in the flour-semolina mixture. Fry the carp halves in portions, putting them head first (so that the tails are at the top) in the bubbling fat. Fry for 10–15 minutes on both sides until golden brown.

5 Remove the fish from the fat with a skimming ladle, drain thoroughly on kitchen paper towel and serve.

Accompaniment: This dish is delicious with a South German potato salad (page 9). In this case the potato salad is prepared without any bacon but with the addition of half a cucumber and two radishes. First rinse the cucumber, wipe dry, cut in half lengthways and remove the seeds. Clean the radishes, rinse and pat dry; then cut into thin slices. Add both to the salad and mix well. If you like, sprinkle freshly chopped parsley and/or chopped chives on the salad before serving. Instead of a potato salad, you can also serve this dish with boiled potatoes and/or a green salad.

Tip: Garnish the carp with slices of organic lemons. Accompany the carp with a strong black beer, or white wine – ideally from Franconia.

Baked Aischgründ carp

Aischgründer Karpfen, gebacken

Delicious with a glass of white wine
or a cold, dark beer.

Picturesque boathouses in the Mecklenburg Lake District

Zander with creamed sauerkraut

Zander mit Rahmkraut with alcohol

Fishing for compliments? With this fish, you'll receive lots

4 servings

For the creamed sauerkraut:

2 onions
1 sharp apple, e. g. Cox's Orange
4 juniper berries, crushed
10 peppercorns
2 bay leaves
50 g/2 oz (3 tbsp) butter
500 g/18 oz sauerkraut
500 ml/17 fl oz (2 cups) dry white wine

For the butter sauce:

1 small onion
80 ml/3 fl oz (3/8 cup) dry white wine
150 ml/5 fl oz (5/8 cup) vegetable or fish stock
200 g/7 oz cream
100 g/3 ½ oz (½ cup) ice-cold butter
salt
freshly ground black pepper

150 g/5 oz crème fraîche
1 pinch sugar

4 zander medallions with skin (each about 150 g–160 g/5–5 ½ oz)
2 tbsp vegetable oil, e. g. sunflower oil

Preparation time: 25–30 minutes
Cooking time: 40–45 minutes

1 To make the creamed sauerkraut, peel and finely chop the onions. Peel the apple, cut into quarters, remove the core and grate coarsely on a kitchen grater. Press the juniper berries and put in a tea infuser (ball). Close the tea infuser.

2 Melt the butter in a pan. Add the chopped onions and fry until transparent. Then add the grated apple, sauerkraut and wine. Place the tea infuser in the middle. Cover and cook over medium heat for about 30 minutes, stirring occasionally.

3 Meanwhile make the butter sauce. Peel and finely chop the onion. Add the chopped onion to the white wine, stock and cream mixture and bring to the boil. Reduce the sauce to one-quarter of its original quantity, then blend with a stick blender. Cut the butter into big cubes, stir into the sauce with a whisk, then season with salt and pepper. Cover and put the sauce in a warm place but do not bring to the boil again since it would curdle.

4 Remove the tea infuser. Stir the crème fraîche into the sauerkraut and cook for another 10 minutes without lid. Season the creamed sauerkraut with salt, pepper and sugar.

5 Rinse the zander medallions under cold running water, pat dry, then season with salt and pepper.

6 Heat the oil in a pan. Add the zander medallions and fry over medium heat, first on the side with the skin, for 2–3 minutes, then on the inner side for about 1 ½ minutes until golden yellow.

7 Serve the zander medallions with the creamed sauerkraut and butter sauce.

Accompaniment: Boiled potatoes

Kale can be harvested in the winter

Kale with smoked pork and pinkel sausages

Grünkohl mit Kasseler und Pinkel

Good for surviving freezing nights wherever they are

4 servings
4 litres/1 gallon (16 cups) water
4 tsp salt
1.5 kg/3 ¼ lb kale
2 onions
100 g/3 ½ oz (½ cup) lard
2 tbsp oatmeal
500 g/18 oz smoked pork loin
250 g/9 oz streaky bacon
375 ml/12 fl oz (1 ½ cups) water
salt
4 smoked pinkel sausages
freshly ground black pepper
grated nutmeg
1 pinch sugar

Preparation time: 40 minutes, excl. cooling time
Cooking time: 1 hour and 20 minutes

1 Put the water in a large pan, cover and bring to the boil, then add salt. Meanwhile remove the outer leaves of the kale and the ribs. Wash the kale thoroughly and drain. Add the kale in portions to the salted boiling water, bring to the boil and blanch for 1–2 minutes. Then put in cold water, leave to drain in a sieve and cool a little. Now coarsely chop the kale.

2 Peel and chop the onions. Melt the clarified butter in a large pan. Add the chopped onions and fry until transparent, then add the chopped kale.

3 Stir in the oat flakes and cook. Rinse the pork, pat dry with kitchen paper towel and remove the bone. Now add the meat and the bone to the pan with the kale. Add the bacon and water, season with salt, bring to the boil, cover and cook for about 1 hour.

4 Now add the sausages to the kale, cover and cook for another 20 minutes.

5 Remove the meat, bone and sausages from the pan and put in a warm place.

6 Season the kale with salt and pepper, nutmeg and sugar. Cut the meat and bacon into slices, then arrange on a large dish with the sausages and kale.

Accompaniment: Boiled or fried potatoes.

Maultaschen mit Spinatfüllung

Ravioli with spinach filling

Swabian ravioli: make them, cook them and enjoy them

4 servings (24 pieces)

In advance:

600 g/1 ¼ lb frozen leaf spinach

For the dough:

300 g/12 oz (2 ½ cups) plain (all purpose) flour
3 eggs (medium)
1 tbsp cooking oil, e. g. sunflower oil
½ tsp salt
some water (if needed)

For the spinach filling:

2 onions
2 cloves garlic
2 tbsp cooking oil, e. g. sunflower or olive oil
salt
freshly ground pepper
ground nutmeg
1 egg yolk (medium)
1 egg white (medium)
about 3 litres/5 ¼ pints (12 cups) vegetable or meat stock
3–4 tbsp chopped chives

Preparation time: about 75 minutes, excl. defrosting and rising time
Cooking time: about 15 minutes

The New Palace, Stuttgart

1 In advance defrost the frozen spinach following the instructions on the packet.

2 For the dough, put the flour in a mixing bowl. Add the eggs, oil and salt. Mix all the ingredients using a hand-mixer with dough hook attachment, first briefly on the lowest setting, then on the highest setting for about 3 minutes until the dough is completely smooth and homogenous, adding a little water if necessary. Cover the dough with a cloth and leave to rise for about 40 minutes.

3 Meanwhile make the spinach filling. Squeeze out all the water from the thawed spinach and chop coarsely. Peel and chop the onions and cloves of garlic.

4 Heat the oil in a pan. Add the chopped onions and cloves of garlic and fry while stirring. Now add the chopped spinach. Cover and continue cooking over low heat for about 3 minutes. Season with salt, pepper and nutmeg, then leave to cool slightly. Finally stir in the egg yolk.

5 Roll out the dough thinly on a well floured work surface to make a rectangle of at least 40 x 60 cm/16 x 24 in. With a pastry wheel cut out squares of 10 x 10 cm/4 x 4 in. Put a portion of filling on each square. Beat the egg white with a fork and brush along the edges of the squares. Fold the squares to make triangles and press the edges together to seal them.

6 Heat the vegetable or meat stock in a large pan. Add the ravioli a few at a time and cook without a lid over low to medium heat for about 15 minutes. When they are cooked, remove them from the stock with a skimming ladle and keep in a warm place. Cook the remaining ravioli in the same way.

7 Serve the ravioli in soup bowls with a little stock and chopped chives.

Tips: Drain the ravioli thoroughly and fry on both sides in melted butter. Then before serving sprinkle with breadcrumbs fried in butter and onion rings (from 6–8 onions) fried in clarified butter or oil.
You can also roll out the pasta dough with a pasta machine. Cooked ravioli are suitable for freezing.

Broad beans with bacon

Dicke Bohnen mit Speck

A tasty, hearty meal from the Rhineland

4 servings
500 g/18 oz freshly podded broad beans (2½–3 kg/5 lb 8 oz–6 lb 10 oz with pods)
1 sprig savory
100 g/3½ oz streaky bacon
2–3 onions
at least 125 ml/4 fl oz (½ cup) water
salt
freshly ground black pepper
1 tbsp chopped chives

Preparation time: 15 minutes
Cooking time: about 40 minutes

1 Rinse the broad beans and savory and pat dry. Cut the bacon into dice.

2 Heat a pan, add the diced bacon and allow the fat to be rendered. Peel the onions, cut into halves and then into slices. Add the sliced onions to the bacon in the pan and fry until golden yellow. Then add the broad beans and continue cooking.

3 Add the savory, season with salt and pepper. Cook for another 40 minutes. Sprinkle the broad beans and diced bacon with chopped chives before serving.

Accompaniment: Streaky bacon, sliced and fried until crisp and brown.

Working in the fresh air makes you hungry

Farmer's breakfast

Bauernfrühstück

There's no better preparation for a hard day

4 servings
750 g/1 lb 10 oz waxy potatoes
4 onions
75g/3 oz streaky bacon
30 g/1 oz (2 tbsp) margarine
or 3 tbsp cooking oil
3 eggs (medium)
3 tbsp milk
salt
freshly ground black pepper
sweet paprika powder
grated nutmeg
125 g/4 ½ oz bacon
2 tbsp chopped chives

Preparation time: 35 minutes, excl. cooling time

1 Brush the potatoes under running water, put in a pan and add water to cover. Put a lid on the pan, bring to the boil and cook for about 20 minutes. Drain the potatoes, plunge in cold water and drain. Peel the potatoes while still warm. Cut the potatoes into slices.

2 Peel and finely chop the onions. Cut the bacon into small cubes. Add the diced bacon to a pan for the fat to be rendered. Add the margarine or cooking oil and heat up. Now add the chopped onions and fry until transparent. Add the sliced potatoes and fry until golden brown.

3 Whisk together the eggs and milk, season with salt, pepper, paprika and nutmeg. Cut the gammon into cubes and stir into the egg-milk mixture together with the chopped chives and pour over the fried potatoes. Allow the egg-milk mixture to thicken over medium heat, turning once.

4 Arrange the farmer's breakfast on a dish and serve immediately.

Variation: To make traditional **fried potatoes,** boil 1 kg/2 ¼ lb firm potatoes as explained in step 1, peel and cut into slices. Heat 5–7 tbsp cooking oil in a large pan. Add the sliced potatoes and season with salt and pepper. Fry the potatoes over low to medium heat, turning occasionally, for about 15 minutes until golden brown. Meanwhile peel and finely chop the onions. Add to the pan with the potatoes and fry for 2 minutes more. Season the fried potatoes with salt and pepper and sprinkle with chopped chives.

Käsespätzle

Very Swabian. Very tasty. Very good.

Vineyards on the slopes of the Hessigheimer Felsengärten

4 servings
3 onions
30 g/1 oz (2 tbsp) butter or margarine

For the spaetzle:
250 g/9 oz plain (all purpose) flour
3 eggs (medium)
½ tsp salt
1 pinch grated nutmeg
about 100 ml/3 ½ fl oz (⅜ cup) water or milk
3 litres/5 ¼ pints (12 cups) water
3 tsp salt
200 g/7 oz (2 cups) grated Emmental
2–3 tbsp chopped chives

Preparation time: 40 minutes
Cooking/baking time: 23–25 minutes

1 Peel the onion, cut into slices, then separate into rings. Melt the butter or margarine in a pan. Add the onion rings and fry until brown, stirring all the time, then arrange on a dish.

2 Preheat the oven:
Top/bottom heat: about 200 °C/400 °F (Gas mark 6)
Fan oven: about 180 °C/350 °F

3 To make the spätzle, pour the flour into a mixing bowl. Add the eggs, salt, nutmeg and water or milk. Mix the ingredients carefully with a wooden spoon, making sure that there are no lumps. Continue mixing the dough until it acquires an elastic, semi-liquid consistency and forms bubbles.

4 Pour the water into a large pan, cover and bring to the boil. Add the salt. Put the dough in portions in the salted boiling water using a spaetzle maker or spaetzle press and cook for 3–5 minutes (the spaetzle are done when they float to the surface).

5 Remove the cooked spaetzle from the water with a skimming ladle, place in a sieve, plunge into cold water and leave to drain.

6 Now arrange the spaetzle and cheese in alternate layers in a gratin dish. The last layer should be cheese. Put the gratin dish on the middle shelf of the preheated oven. Bake the cheese spaetzle for about 20 minutes.

7 Sprinkle the fried onion rings and chopped chives on the cheese spaetzle before serving.

Accompaniment: A mixed salad.

Finger dumplings

Schupfnudeln

The German-speaking answer
to Italian gnocchi

The historic old town of Nürtingen between the Neckar valley and the Swabian Alps

4 servings – 36 pieces
300 g/10 oz floury potatoes
salt
1 egg (medium)
100 g/3 ½ oz (generous ¾ cup) plain (all purpose) flour
freshly ground pepper
ground nutmeg
salted water: 1 litre/1 ¾ pints (4 cups) water
with 1 tsp salt
30 g/1 oz (2 tbsp) butter

Preparation time: about 25 minutes,
excl. cooling time
Cooking time for the potatoes: about 20 minutes
Cooking time for the dumplings: 6–8 minutes

1 Peel the potatoes, rinse and leave to drain. Put the potatoes in a pan, add water to cover them, put a lid on the pan, then bring to the boil. Add salt and cook for about 20 minutes. Pour away the water, dry the potatoes and push through a potato ricer or mash with a potato masher and leave to cool.

2 Knead the potatoes together with the egg, flour, salt, pepper and nutmeg in a mixing bowl. Mix the ingredients using a hand-mixer with dough hook attachment. Then transfer onto a floured work surface and knead into a smooth dough. With flour-covered hands, make finger-thick rolls about 5 cm/2 in long, then roll the ends a bit more to make them slightly thinner.

3 Bring enough salted water to the boil so that the dumplings can "swim" in the water. Put the dumplings in the boiling salted water, bring back to the boil and cook without a lid over low heat for 3–4 minutes (the water must move only very slightly).

4 Remove the finger dumplings from the water with a skimming ladle and drain well. Melt the butter. Add the finger dumplings and cook for 3–4 minutes, stirring occasionally.

Tip: Serve finger dumplings with, braised beef, goulash, sautéd strips of meat or sauerkraut.

Rahmschwammerl mit Semmelknödeln

Bavarian delights

4–6 servings

For the dumplings:

50 g/2 oz streaky bacon
2 onions
1 tbsp cooking oil, e. g. sunflower oil
300 g (about 8) day-old bread rolls
300 ml/10 fl oz (1 ¼ cups) milk
30 g/1 oz (2 tbsp) butter
4 eggs (medium)
2 tbsp chopped parsley
salt
salted water: 1 tsp salt
in 1 litre/1 ¾ pints (4 cups) water

For the mushrooms in cream sauce:

800 g/1 lb 12 oz mixed mushrooms, e. g. chanterelles, button mushrooms, oyster mushrooms, porcini
1 onion
2 tbsp clarified butter or sunflower oil
freshly ground black pepper
15 g/½ oz (2 tbsp) flour
300 g/10 oz whipping cream
grated zest of ½ organic lemon (untreated, unwaxed)
150 g/5 oz crème fraîche
3 tbsp chopped parsley

Preparation time: 50 minutes, excl. cooling time

ushrooms in a cream sauce

1 To make the dumplings, cut the bacon into dice. Peel and finely chop the onions. Heat the oil in a pan. Add the diced bacon and fry until crisp. Now add the chopped onions and continue frying over low heat, stirring all the time.

2 Cut the rolls into small cubes and put in a bowl. Heat the milk together with the butter, then pour over the cubed rolls and mix well. Now stir the bacon-onion mixed with the frying fat into the softened cubed rolls and milk mixture, then leave to cool.

3 Whisk together the parsley and eggs, stir into the cooled rolls and milk mixture, then season with salt. Coat your hands with flour and form the mixture into 12 dumplings. Fill a large pan with enough water for the dumplings to "swim" in it, add salt and bring to the boil. Put the dumplings in the salted boiling water, bring to the boil again and simmer for about 20 minutes (the water must only move slightly).

4 Meanwhile, for the mushroom and cream sauce, clean the mushrooms, rinse them if necessary and pat dry. Cut the mushrooms into large pieces. Peel and finely chop the onion. Heat the clarified butter or oil in a large pan. Add the chopped onion, fry until golden, then add the mushrooms and continue frying until they become slightly shiny. Season the mushroom mixture with salt and pepper.

5 Sprinkle the mushrooms with flour and stir until you cannot see the flour any more. Then add the cream and lemon zest and simmer lightly for 3–4 minutes.

6 Finally stir in the crème fraîche and 2 tbsp parsley, bring briefly to the boil again and season again with salt and pepper to taste.

7 Remove the cooked dumplings from the water with a skimming ladle and leave to drain thoroughly.

8 Arrange the mushroom and cream sauce with the dumplings on a plate and sprinkle with parsley.

Tips: These dumplings also very delicious served with roasts.
The rolls should be left to become stale for 2–3 days before making these "white bread" dumplings.

Variation: For **pretzel dumplings,** replace the white rolls with Laugengebäck (pretzel baked goods) and stir 1 tbsp chopped chives into the dumpling mixture.

Gekochte Kartoffelklöße (on the right)

Boiled potato dumplings

As soon as they float to the surface, serve them

4 servings (12 pieces)
750 g/1 lb 10 oz floury potatoes
50 g/2 oz (1 cup) breadcrumbs
20 g plain (all purpose) flour
2 eggs (medium)
salt
grated nutmeg
salted water: 1 tsp salt in 1 litre/1 ¾ pints (4 cups) water

Preparation time: 40 minutes (spread over 2 days), excl. cooling time
Standing time for the potatoes: about 20 minutes
Standing time for the dumplings: about 20 minutes

1 Brush the potatoes under cold running water, add just enough water to cover the potatoes, put a lid on the pan, bring to the boil and cook for about 20 minutes. Drain the potatoes, plunge in cold water, then drain. Peel the potatoes while still warm, push immediately through a potato press or mash with a potato masher, leave to cool, cover and leave overnight in the refrigerator.

2 Stir the breadcrumbs, flour and eggs into the potato mixture with a mixer (with kneading hook attachment) or with a mixing spoon, season with salt and nutmeg. With flour-coated hands, make 12 dumplings.

3 Fill a large pan with enough water for the dumplings to "swim", add salt and bring to the boil. Put the dumplings in the boiling water, bring to the boil again and simmer for 20 minutes without a lid (the water must only move very slightly). Take the cooked dumplings out of the water with a skimming ladle and drain thoroughly.

Variations: To make **half-and-half potato dumplings** (top left), first prepare 750 g/1 lb 10 oz floury potatoes as described in step 1 and leave in the refrigerator overnight. Then peel 500 g/18 oz floury potatoes, rinse and grate into a bowl filled cold water. Pour the grated potatoes into a sieve, squeeze dry with a dish towel and add to the boiled potatoes. Now knead 1 egg (medium), 65 g/2 ¼ oz (½ cup) plain (all purpose) flour and 1 level tsp salt into the potatoes. With flour-coated hands, make 12 dumplings and cook as described in step 3.

To make **raw potato dumplings** (bottom left), peel 1.5 kg/3 ¼ lb floury potatoes, rinse, drain and grate into a bowl filled with cold water. Line a sieve with a dish towel, transfer the grated potatoes into it, twist the dish towel and squeeze well. Now put these squeezed-dry grated potatoes into a mixing bowl. Bring 250 ml/8 fl oz (1 cup) milk together with 40 g/1 ½ oz (3 tbsp) butter or margarine and 2 level tsp salt to the boil. Sprinkle 150 g/5 oz (scant 1 cup) semolina (made from durum wheat) into the milk and bring to the boil, stirring all the time. Then pour the milk-semolina mixture onto the squeeze-dry grated potatoes. Mix all the ingredients with a hand-mixer (with kneading hook attachment) until you obtain a smooth consistency. Season the mixture again with salt. Cut 1 bread roll into small cubes. Melt 30 g/1 oz (2 tbsp) butter or margarine in a pan, add the cubed roll and fry until golden brown, stirring occasionally. Then make 12 dumplings from the potato mixture and press several fried cubes into each dumpling. Cook the dumplings as described in step 3.

Tip: Serve the potato dumplings with meat dishes in a sauce, for instance roast pork, marinated beef or beef roulade.

Potato pancakes

Reibekuchen

Extremely popular all over Germany – both at home and as street food

4 servings

1 kg/2 ¼ lb waxy potatoes
1 onion
3 eggs (medium)
1 level tsp salt
freshly ground black pepper
grated nutmeg
40 g/1 ¼ oz (⅓ cup) plain (all purpose) flour
100 ml/3 ½ fl oz (⅜ cup) cooking oil,
e. g. sunflower oil

Preparation time: 45 minutes

1 Peel the potatoes, rinse and drain. Peel the onion. Grate potatoes and onion coarsely on a kitchen grater. If necessary, squeeze out excess moisture.

2 Stir the eggs, salt, pepper, nutmeg and flour into the potato-onion mixture and mix thoroughly.

3 Heat a little of the oil in a non-stick pan. Add the potato-flour dough in portions to the pan, using a sauce ladle or large spoon. Press the dough flat with the back of a spoon and fry on both sides until the edges turn crispy brown. Take the pancakes out of the pan and place on kitchen paper towel.

4 Pat away excess fat with kitchen paper towel. Serve the potato pancakes immediately or keep in a warm place. Continue making the potato pancakes in the same way with the rest of the dough.

Tip: If you replace half the flour with oat flakes, the pancakes will be even crispier.
Serve the potato pancakes with a little crème fraîche and 100 g/3 ½ oz ham, cut into strips.
You can also serve stewed apples or apple compote as a side dish with the pancakes.
Try the potato pancakes cold with bread and butter.

Heaven and earth with black pudding

Himmel und Erde mit Blutwurst

A perfect match: apples of heaven and potatoes of the earth

4 servings
800 g/1 lb 12 oz floury potatoes
salt
500 g/18 oz apples
1 tbsp sugar
200–250 ml/7–8 fl oz (¾–1 cup) milk
grated zest of ½ organic lemon (untreated, unwaxed)
30 g/1 oz (2 tbsp) butter
freshly ground black pepper
grated nutmeg
100 g/3½ oz bacon
2 onions
500 g/18 oz black pudding (blutwurst)
a little flour
2 tbsp sunflower oil

Preparation time: 20 minutes
Cooking time: about 35 minutes

Cologne Cathedral:
a World Heritage Site with a soul

1 Peel the potatoes, rinse, drain and cut into small cubes. Add enough water to cover the potatoes, put a lid on the pan and bring to the boil. Add salt. Cook the cubed potatoes for about 15 minutes.

2 Meanwhile, peel the apples, cut into quarters, core and cut into cubes of about 1 cm/⅜ in. Put the cubed apples in the pan together with sugar, cover and cook over medium heat until soft.

3 Drain the potatoes in a sieve and mash with a potato masher. Heat the milk. Mix the potatoes with the apples, milk, lemon zest and butter. Season the potato-apple mixture with salt, pepper and nutmeg.

4 Cut the bacon into dice. Peel the onions, cut first into slices, then divide into rings. Heat a pan, add the bacon and fry to render the fat out. Then add the onion rings and fry until golden brown.

5 Cut the black pudding into slices about 1 cm/⅜ in thick and coat in flour. Heat the oil in a pan, add the black pudding slices and fry on both sides. Serve the potatoes-apple mash with the fried black pudding slices and fried bacon-onion mixture.

Tips: You can also serve "Heaven and Earth" with fried liver, boiled sausages, roast duck or game. You can put the potatoes through a potato press and then mix with the apples.

Frankfurt green sauce

Frankfurter Grüne Sauce

Seven herbs for the greenest sauce of all

4 servings
about 150 g/5 oz fresh herbs for Frankfurt green sauce
150 g/5 oz crème fraîche or sour cream
1 small onion
150 g/5 oz yoghurt
1–2 tbsp olive oil
1 tsp medium mustard
1 drop lemon juice
½ tsp sugar
salt
freshly ground pepper

Preparation time: 20 minutes

Frankfurt am Main is also known as "Mainhattan"

1 Rinse the herbs, pat dry and remove the leaves from the stems. Chop the leaves coarsely and purée together with 2 tbsp crème fraîche or sour cream in a bowl; alternatively chop the herbs very finely and stir together with the crème fraîche or the sour cream. Peel and finely chop the onions.

2 Stir the rest of the crème fraîche or sour cream, yoghurt, chopped onions, oil and mustard into the herb-crème fraîche mixture or the herbs. Season the sauce with lemon juice, sugar, salt and pepper and refrigerate, covered, until ready to serve.

Uses: Serve Frankfurt green sauce with new potatoes and hard-boiled eggs or with boiled beef.

Tip: The "authentic" Frankfurt green sauce is made with 7 fresh herbs. But depending on the season the composition can vary. In some place bags of ready-to-use mixed herbs (about 150 g/5 oz) for making Frankfurt green sauce are available. Otherwise you can use a bunch of mixed herbs such as parsley, chives, chervil, burnet, borage, lemon balm and watercress or sorrel. You can also use frozen herbs.

Marinated sour milk cheese

Handkäs mit Musik

The sour milk cheese snack from Hesse, perfect with cider

4 servings
400 g/14 oz (2 rolls) Harzer cheese

For the marinade:
6 tbsp cooking oil
8 tbsp vinegar
salt
freshly ground black pepper
caraway seeds
2 onions
1 tbsp finely chopped flat-leaved parsley
a little coarsely ground black pepper

Preparation time: 15 minutes, excl. marinating time

1 Cut the Harzer cheese into 8 slices and put in a ceramic or earthenware bowl.

2 For the marinade, whisk together the oil with the vinegar, salt, pepper and caraway seeds.

3 Peel the onions, cut in half, then into small cubes. Stir the cubed onions into the marinade. Pour the marinade over the cheese and leave to stand for about 12 hours.

4 Sprinkle the cheese with parsley and coarsely ground pepper before serving.

Accompaniment: Fresh, nourishing farmhouse bread with butter

Tip: Delicious with a traditional cider.

The Römer in Frankfurt – a famous landmark and the city hall

Obatzter

Bavarian cheese spread

Mix and mash for the Bavarian beer garden atmosphere

about 550 g/20 oz
4 Camembert cheeses (each 125 g/4 ½ oz, 45% fat)
50 g/2 oz (3 tbsp) butter (room temperature)
1 onion
1 tbsp whole caraway seeds
salt
freshly ground black pepper
a little sweet paprika powder

Preparation time: 30 minutes

Beer and snacks beneath the chestnut trees: what a beer garden should be.

1 Cut the Camembert into pieces and put in a bowl. Add the butter. Mash together the butter and Camembert pieces with a fork.

2 Peel the onion, cut in half and then into small cubes. Knead the cubed onion and caraway into the cheese mixture. Season with salt, pepper and paprika. Put the cheese spread in a sealable container and store in the refrigerator.

Tips: To serve: Peel 1 onion, cut into rings and coat in paprika. Garnish the Obatzter with the paprika-coated onion rings and a few parsley leaves. The spread will keep for about 3 days in the refrigerator.
To make a a slightly milder, creamier spread, stir in about 100 g/3 ½ oz cream cheese.

Buchteln

A sweet Bohemian export to Austro-Bavarian cuisine

The picturesque city of Český Krumlov on a loop of the Vltava river in Bohemia

12 pieces

For the dough:
250 ml/8 fl oz (1 cup) milk
75 g/2 ½ oz (⅓ cup) butter or margarine
500 g plain (all purpose) flour
1 sachet dried yeast
50 g/2 oz (¼ cup) sugar
1 sachet vanilla sugar
4 drops lemon aroma
1 pinch salt
1 egg (medium)

For coating:
50 g/2 oz (3 tbsp) butter

For sprinkling:
some icing (confectioners') sugar

Preparation time: 25 minutes, excl. rising time
Baking time: about 25 minutes

1 For the dough, heat up the milk in a small pan. Melt the butter or margarine in it.

2 Put the flour in a mixing bowl and stir in the dry yeast, making sure it is well mixed in. Now add the sugar, vanilla sugar, flavouring, salt, egg and the warm milk and butter or margarine mixture. Mix together all the ingredients with a mixer (kneading hook) briefly on the lowest setting, then on the highest setting for about 5 minutes until the dough mixture is completely smooth. Then cover the dough and place in a warm place until it has visibly increased in volume.

3 Preheat the oven:
Top/bottom heat: about 200 °C/400 °F (Gas mark 6)
Fan oven: about 180 °C/350 °F

4 Knead the dough again briefly on a lightly floured work surface, then shape into a cylinder and cut into 12 pieces of similar size. Shape the pieces into small balls and arrange them in a (greased) soufflé dish, not too close together.

5 For coating the dumplings, melt the butter and brush the dumplings with it, then and put them again in a warm place until they have further increased in volume. Put the soufflé dish on the middle shelf of the preheated oven and bake the dumplings for about 25 minutes.

6 Sprinkle the yeast dumplings with icing (confectioner's) sugar and serve warm.

Tip: Serve with compote and warm vanilla sauce.

Variation: For **yeast dumplings with plum jam filling,** flatten each dumpling, place 1 tsp plum jam on each one, wrap the dough round it and shape it into a ball again.

The rhubarb harvest season traditionally ends on Midsummer in June

Bread pudding with rhubarb

Rhabarber-Ofenschlupfer with alcohol

One of the best ways to use a brioche – and rhubarb

4 servings
300 g/10 oz brioche
250 g/9 oz rhubarb
120 g/4 ½ oz (⅝ cup) sugar
50 g/2 oz (scant ½ cup) raisins or currants
50 ml/1 ½ fl oz (3 tbsp) rum
50g/2 oz (scant ½ cup) slivered almonds
1 vanilla pod
4 eggs (medium)
200 g/7 oz whipping cream
300 ml/10 fl oz (1 ¼ cups) milk
½ level tsp ground cinnamon
1 pinch salt

some breadcrumbs for sprinkling on the mould

Preparation time: 20 minutes, excl. drying time
Baking time: about 20 minutes

1 Cut the brioche into 1 cm/⅜ in cubes and leave to dry overnight (e. g. on a baking sheet).

2 Clean the rhubarb, peel, rinse, drain and cut into small pieces. Put the rhubarb in a bowl with sugar.

3 Put the raisins or currants with the rum in a pan and bring briefly to the boil. Remove the pan from the heat.

4 Put the slivered almonds in a pan without fat and roast until golden brown, stirring all the while, then put them on a plate.

5 Cut the vanilla pod open lengthways and scrape out the pulp.

6 Preheat the oven:
Top/bottom heat: about 200 °C/400 °F (Gas mark 6)
Fan oven: about 180 °C/350 °F
Fill a roasting pan with water about 1 cm/⅜ in deep and put in the oven on the middle shelf.

7 Whisk the eggs with the cream and milk. Stir in the vanilla pulp. Season the mixture with cinnamon and salt.

8 Now stir together the cubed brioche, pieces of rhubarb and the raisins or currants with rum. Spoon this mixture into a soufflé dish (about 25 x 30 cm/10 x 12 in, greased and coated in breadcrumbs). Now pour the egg-cream mixture evenly over the brioche mixture. Sprinkle the slivered almonds on top.

9 Place the soufflé dish in the roasting pan with water and return to the preheated oven. Bake for about 20 minutes.

Tips: Serve the bread pudding with a vanilla sauce. When rhubarb is out of season you can use fresh berries or fresh stone fruits instead.

Kirschmichel

Cherry dreams come true in this traditional baked pudding of bread, milk, eggs and cherries

4 servings
2 day-old milk rolls or croissants
125 ml/4 fl oz (½ cup) milk
370 g/13 oz drained sour cherries (from the jar)
125 g/4 ½ oz (⅝ cup) sugar
3 egg yolks (medium)
2 tbsp butter
1 sachet vanilla sugar
zest of ½ organic lemon (untreated, unwaxed)
3 egg whites (medium)
1 pinch salt
50g/2 oz (scant ½ cup) slivered almonds
a little icing (confectioners') sugar or granulated sugar

Preparation time: 15 minutes
Baking time: about 40 minutes

The cherry blossom festival is celebrated not only in Japan but in Germany as well.

1 Cut the rolls into thin slices, put in a bowl and pour the milk on top. Mix together the cherries and half the sugar.

2 Preheat the oven:
Top/bottom heat: about 200 °C/400 °F (Gas mark 6)
Fan oven: about 180 °C/350 °F

3 Whisk the egg yolk together with 1 tbsp butter, the rest of the sugar and vanilla sugar until foamy. Mix together the softened slices of rolls with the milk and the lemon zest and continue stirring until the slices have completely disintegrated.

4 Beat the egg whites with salt until they form peaks and carefully fold into the mixture together with the cherries. Spoon this mixture into a greased soufflé dish. Cut the rest of the butter into small pieces, scatter over the mixture and sprinkle with slivered almonds.

5 Put the dish on a shelf in the preheated oven and bake for about 40 minutes.

6 Sprinkle icing (confectioner's) sugar or castor sugar on the cherry pudding while it is still warm and serve immediately.

Tip: This is particularly delicious with some lightly whipped cream.

Baked apples

Bratäpfel with alcohol

Even more delicious with warm vanilla sauce.

Baked apples taste best when it is really very cold.

8 servings

1 tbsp raisins
about 100 ml/3 ½ fl oz (⅜ cup) rum
8 apples, e. g. Holsteiner Cox or Boskop
20 g/ ¾ oz (1 ½ tbsp) butter (room temperature)
20 g/ ¾ oz (1 ½ tbsp) sugar
1 sachet vanilla sugar
2 tbsp ground almonds
2 tbsp slivered almonds

Preparation time: 20 minutes, excl. soaking time
Cooking time: about 40 minutes

1 Put the raisins in 2 tbsp rum, cover and soak overnight.

2 Preheat the oven:
Top/bottom heat: about 200 °C/400 °F (Gas mark 6)
Fan oven: about 180 °C/350 °F

3 Remove the stalks from the apples, wash in hot water and wipe dry. Remove the core with an apple-corer, starting from the peduncle but do not go through completely. Arrange the apples in a greased soufflé dish.

4 With a spoon stir together the butter, sugar, vanilla sugar, ground almonds and raisins soaked in rum and stuff the apples with this mixture, using a teaspoon. Sprinkle almond slivers on top and press lightly into the filling. Pour the rest of the rum round the apples in the soufflé dish.

5 Put the soufflé dish on the lowest shelf in the preheated oven and bake for about 40 minutes.

6 Take the baked apples out of the oven and serve hot.

Tips: Serve the baked apples sprinkled with icing (confectioner's) sugar, with vanilla sauce or lightly whipped cream. Baked apples make an ideal dessert but they are also delicious as a tea-time snack.

Variation: For **baked apples without alcohol**, soak the raisins in 2 tbsp orange or apple juice, drain, then use as described in the recipe. And instead of the rum, pour orange or apple juice round the apples in the dish before baking.

Salzburger Nockerln

An Austrian soufflé, light as a feather and sweet as a kiss

3–4 servings
4 egg yolks (medium)
2 tbsp plain (all purpose) flour
1 pinch cornflour (cornstarch)
1 pinch salt
3 drops vanilla flavouring
4 egg whites (medium)
2 tbsp caster (superfine) sugar
2 tbsp icing (confectioners') sugar

Preparation time: 20 minutes
Baking time: about 10 minutes

View of the castle dominating Mozart's city of Salzburg

1 Preheat the oven:
Top/bottom heat: about 200 °C/400 °F (Gas mark 6)
Fan oven: about 180 °C/350 °F

2 Mix together the egg yolks, flour, cornflour (cornstarch), salt and flavouring. Using a hand-held mixer, whisk the egg whites on the highest setting but only until they become creamy. Then whisk in the sugar little by little.

3 Carefully stir 1 tbsp beaten egg white into the egg yolk and flour mixture, then fold the egg yolk and flour mixture into the rest of the beaten egg whites.

4 Arrange the mixture in three heaps on a flat greased soufflé dish. Put the dish on the middle shelf in the preheated oven. Bake the soufflés for about 10 minutes, when the tips should be lightly brown.
Sprinkle the soufflé with icing (confectioner's) sugar and serve immediately.

Accompaniment: These soufflés are particularly delicious with home-made **raspberry sauce:** Mix 300 g/10 oz raspberries with 30–50 g/1–2 oz (2½ tbsp–¼ cup) sugar and some lemon juice, then rub through a sieve.

Tip: These soufflés collapse very quickly because they are only brown on the outside, they should still be soft and moist inside.

Advice: Only use very fresh eggs which not older than five days (check the laying date).

Yeast dumplin

Hefeklöße

A reminder of grandmother's kitchen

8 pieces

125 ml/4 fl oz (½ cup) milk
50 g/2 oz (4 tbsp) butter or margarine
300 g/12 oz (2 ½ cups) plain (all purpose) flour
1 packet easy-blend dried yeast
50 g/2 oz (¼ cup) sugar
1 packet vanilla sugar
1 level tsp salt
1 egg (medium)

Preparation time: 20 minutes, excl. rising time
Cooking time: 20–25 minutes

1 Heat the milk in a pan and melt the butter or margarine in it. Put the flour in a mixing bowl, stir in the dried yeast and mix well. Now add the sugar, vanilla sugar, salt, egg and milk-butter or margarine mixture. Mix all the ingredients with a hand-mixer with dough hook attachment, starting briefly on the lowest setting, then using the highest setting for about 5 minutes until you have a smooth, homogenous dough. Cover the bowl and put it in a warm place until the dough has doubled in size, about 40 minutes.

2 Put the dough on a lightly floured surface and knead again briefly. Shape the dough into a cylinder, then cut it into 8 equal pieces. With floury hands, shape these pieces into dumplings and place on a floured board. Cover the dumplings and put in a warm place until they have visibly increased in volume, about 15 minutes.

3 Stretch a cloth tautly over a wide pan filled with boiling water. Secure the cloth round the pan with tape (parcel tape) and sprinkle flour on top. Place the dumplings on the cloth. Then place an inverted heat-resistant bowl over the dumplings as a lid. Be careful: the bowl can become very hot! Cook the dumplings over medium heat for 20–25 minutes (they are done when a wooden skewer poked into the dumplings comes out without any dough sticking to it).

Tip: Serve the yeast dumplings with melted, browned butter, cinnamon sugar and/or fruit compote.

The cathedral and Albrechtsburg castle on the Burgberg hill in Meissen, seen from the River Elbe

4 servings
500 g/18 oz floury potatoes
salt
375 g/13 oz quark
150 g/6 oz (scant 1 ¼ cups) plain (all purpose) flour
50 g/2 oz (¼ cup) sugar
1 sachet vanilla sugar
2 eggs (medium)
grated zest of ½ organic lemon (untreated, unwaxed)
grated zest of ½ organic orange (untreated, unwaxed)
1 pinch ground cinnamon
50 g/2 oz Rum-Raisins filling
some plain (all purpose) flour

For the strawberry-rhubarb compote:
250 g/9 oz strawberries
500 g/18 oz rhubarb
250 ml/8 fl oz (1 cup) water
3–4 tbsp sugar
40 g/1 ½ oz (5 tbsp) custard powder (vanilla pudding mix)
3–4 tbsp clarified butter of cooking oil, e. g. sunflower oil
1 tbsp icing (confectioners') sugar

Preparation time: 35 minutes, excl. cooling
Cooking time (potatoes): about 20 minutes

1 Brush the potatoes under running water, then add just enough water to cover. Put a lid on the pan and cook for about 20 minutes. Drain the potatoes, plunge in cold water and drain again. Peel the potatoes while still warm and immediately push through a potato press or mash with a potato masher. Leave the potatoes to cool.

2 Mix the pressed potatoes with the quark, flour, sugar, vanilla sugar, eggs, lemon and orange zest, cinnamon and 1 pinch of salt, using a hand-held mixer until you obtain a smooth dough. Now carefully work in the rum-raisin filling.

3 Put the dough on a lightly floured work surface and shape into a cylinder 6–8 cm/2 ½–3 in long, then cut this into slices 1.5–2 cm/⅝–¾ in thick. Coat the dough slices lightly in flour.

4 For the compote, rinse the strawberries, leave to drain, remove the stalks and cut in half. Clean the rhubarb, rinse, leave to drain and cut into pieces as thick as a finger.

5 Place the halved strawberries and cut-up rhubarb in a pan. Add water, bring to the boil and cook for about 4 minutes over low heat. Stir in the sugar and adjust if necessary. Stir 4 tbsp water into the vanilla custard powder and stir into the compote. Bring briefly to the boil, stirring all the time. Transfer the compote to a bowl and leave to cool.

6 Now heat some clarified butter or cooking oil in a large pan, add the dough slices in portions and fry on both sides over medium heat until golden brown.

7 Arrange the potato pancakes on a warmed dish and sprinkle with icing (confectioners') sugar. Serve with the rhubarb-strawberry compote.

Tip: These pancakes are also delicious with fruit salad. To make a fruit salad, stir together lemon juice with honey and cut-up the fruit such as apples, pears, bananas, melon or oranges – whatever you have in the house.

Quark potato pancakes with compote

Quarkkeulchen mit Kompott with alcohol

One of Saxony's most famous dishes,
have potatoes ever been so delicious?

Kaiserschmarren

The most legendary of Austrian desserts, shredded pancakes with raisins

2 servings
4 egg whites (medium)
4 egg yolks (medium)
100 g/3 ½ oz (generous ¾ cup) plain (all purpose) flour
1 pinch salt
1 sachet vanilla sugar
200 g/7 oz whipping cream or 200 ml/7 fl oz (¾ cup) milk
50 g/2 oz (scant ½ cup) raisins
about 50 g clarified butter or 4 tbsp cooking oil, e. g. sunflower oil
a little icing (confectioners') sugar

Preparation time: about 30 minutes

The Habsburg Franz Joseph I, Emperor of Austria from 1848 to 1916

1 Beat the egg whites until stiff. Put the egg yolks, flour, salt, vanilla sugar, cream or milk in a mixing bowl. Mix the ingredients with a hand-held mixer until you obtain a smooth dough. Fold in the beaten egg whites and the raisins.

2 Heat a little clarified butter or oil in a pan (diameter 28 cm/11 in). Add half the dough and fry over medium heat until the underside has turned slightly golden. Now cut the dough which is still slightly "runny" on top into quarters using two spatulas, turn over and fry until slightly golden; if necessary, add a little more fat to the pan.

3 Then tear the little pancakes into small pieces, using the spatulas again; arrange the pancake pieces on a plate and keep warm. Prepare the rest of the dough in the same way. Sprinkle with icing (confectioners') sugar before serving.

Tip: Kaiserschmarren can be served as a sweet main dish or as pudding in which case it will serve four; it is delicious accompanied by plum or apricot compote.

Variation 1: Before using the raisins you can soak them in warm, brown rum for about 30 minutes. Work the raisins (with the rum) into the dough as indicated in the recipe.

Variation 2: To make **Kaiserschmarren with nougat,** replace the raisins with 100 g/3 ½ oz chopped-up nougat and 50 g/2 oz chopped almonds and work into the dough. Prepare the Kaiserschmarren as indicated in the recipe.
To make **Kaiserschmarren with apples and sour cherries,** use only 150 ml/5 fl oz (⅝ cup) milk or 150 g/5 oz cream and, instead of the raisins, work 1 grated apple and 75g/3 oz dried sour cherries into the dough. Then prepare the Kaiserschmarren as described in the recipe.

Grießpudding

A sweet finish of your meal – dive in but don't rush it!

4 servings
½ vanilla pod
500 ml/17 fl oz (2 cups) milk
75 g/3 oz (⅓ cup) sugar
grated zest of ½ organic lemon (untreated, unwaxed)
grated zest of ½ organic orange (untreated, unwaxed)
50 g/2 oz (⅓ cup) semolina
1 egg yolk (medium)
1 egg white (medium)

Preparation time: 20 minutes, excl. cooling time

The historic linen weaver fountain in the "Puddingtown" of Bielefeld

1 Cut the vanilla pod open lengthways with a knife and scrape out the pulp. Bring the milk to the boil together with the sugar, grated lemon zest and orange zest, vanilla pod and pulp in a pan. Sprinkle the semolina into the milk while stirring, bring to the boil again and simmer for about 1 minute, stirring all the time.

2 Remove the pan from the heat and remove the vanilla pod. Stir the egg yolk briskly into the semolina mixture. Beat the egg white until stiff and fold into the hot semolina.

3 Pour the semolina pudding into a mould, bowl or individual dishes, all previously rinsed in cold water. Leave to cool, then cover and put in the refrigerator for about 3 hours.

4 Before serving, carefully loosen the edge of the semolina with a knife, then turn over onto a plate.

Tips: Serve semolina pudding with rhubarb compote, fresh fruit and whipped cream or apricot halves.
Because the semolina mixture sometimes bubbles and splashes, it is a good idea to use a spoon or whisk with a long handle when stirring.

Variations: To make **semolina-quark cream cheese pudding,** after folding in the stiffly beaten egg white, stir 125 g/4½ oz quark (20 % fat) into the lukewarm pudding (add more sugar to taste).
To make **semolina pudding with cinnamon,** replace the vanilla pod with a cinnamon stick.

Advice: Only use very fresh eggs which are not over 5 days old (check the date when they were laid!). Keep the semolina pudding in the refrigerator and consume within 24 hours.

Rice pudding

Milchreis

Nothing goes better with cinnamon and sugar, and it's great hot or cold

6 servings (as dessert)
1 litre/1 ¾ pints (4 cups) milk
1 pinch salt
20 g/ ¾ oz (1 ½ tbsp) sugar
1 sachet vanilla sugar
175 g/6 oz (generous ¾ cup) pudding rice (short grain rice)
2 tbsp sugar
½ level tsp ground cinnamon

Preparation time: 15 minutes
Standing time: about 35 minutes

1 Bring the milk with salt, sugar and vanilla sugar to the boil, stirring occasionally.

2 Stir in the rice and bring to the boil again, while still stirring; put the lid half on and simmer over low heat for about 35 minutes, stirring occasionally so that the rice does not burn.

3 Sprinkle sugar and cinnamon on the rice pudding while warm if served immediately; if it is to be served cold, sprinkle with sugar and cinnamon just before serving.

Tips: If you like you can also add a small piece of lemon zest (from untreated, unwaxed lemon, previously washed under warm running water) to cook with the rice.
As a main course the rice pudding will serve 3–4 people.

This was the favourite dessert of Elector Ernest Augustus. Today people in Hanover meet "under the tail" of his statue

Welfenspeise with alcohol

A sophisticated temptation from Lower Saxony in the white and yellow Guelph colours

4 servings

For the cream:

2 egg whites (medium)
35 g/¼ oz (¼ cup) cornflour (cornstarch)
40 g/1 ½ oz (scant ¼ cup) sugar
1 sachet vanilla sugar
500 ml/17 fl oz (2 cups) milk

For the white wine foam:

3 egg yolks (medium)
80 g/3 oz (generous ⅓ cup) sugar
10 g/⅓ oz (5 tsp) cornflour (cornstarch)
250 ml/8 fl oz (1 cup) white wine

Preparation time: 30 minutes, excl. cooling time

1 For the cream, beat the egg whites stiff with a hand-held mixer on the highest setting. The egg whites must be firm enough to form stiff peaks. Mix together the cornflour (cornstarch) with the sugar and vanilla sugar. Stir 6 tbsp of the milk into this mixture.

2 Bring the rest of the milk to the boil in a pan. Remove the pan from the heat. With a whisk, stir the cornflour-sugar-milk mixture into the milk in the pan and bring briefly to the boil.

3 Stir the stiffly beaten egg into the hot boiling mixture and bring briefly to the boil again. Pour the mixture into a glass bowl or individual glass ramekins (fill only half-full!), cover and place in the refrigerator.

4 To make the white wine foam, put the egg yolks with the sugar, cornflour and white wine in a stainless steel pan or bowl. Mix the ingredients with a hand-held mixer on the lowest setting in a hot bain-marie until the mixture is foamy through and through (the mixture must more or less double in volume but make sure that the neither the water or the "wine foam" come to the boil or the mixture will curdle). Take the pan or bowl out of the bain-marie, loosen the mixture round the edge and stir briefly again.

5 Leave the wine foam to cool, then carefully spoon onto the cream.

Tip: Garnish the pudding with woodruff or lemon balm leaves before serving.

If you do not want to use alcohol, make an apple-lemon foam instead of the white wine foam. To do this, replace the white wine by 250 ml/8 fl oz (1 cup) apple juice and 3 tbsp lemon juice.

Advice: only use very fresh eggs which are not more than 5 days old (check the laying date!). Keep the pudding in the refrigerator and consume within 24 hours.

Rote Grütze

A refreshing northern dish with heavenly berries and cherries

6 servings
250 g/9 oz each blackberries, red currants, raspberries, strawberries (all fruits well prepared)
35 g/1 ¼ oz cornflour (cornstarch)
100 g/3 ½ oz (½ cup) sugar
500 ml/17 fl oz (2 cups) fruit juice, e. g. morello cherry or red currant juice

Preparation time: about 20 minutes, excl. cooling time

The Westerheversand lighthouse on the Eiderstedt Peninsula in northern Friesland

1 Sort out the blackberries if necessary, removing any damaged ones, rinse gently and leave to drain thoroughly. Wash the red currants, leave to drain thoroughly and strip the currants off the stalks. Sort out the raspberries but do not wash. Wash the strawberries, leave to drain, remove the stalks and, depending on the size of the fruit, cut into halves or quarters.

2 Mix the sugar and cornflour (cornstarch) together, then add 4 tbsp of the juice and stir to obtain a homogenous paste. Put the rest of the juice in a pan. Stir the cornflour mixture into the juice and bring to the boil, then remove the pan from the heat. Stir in the fruit.

3 Put the red fruit jelly in a glass bowl or in individual glass serving dishes and put in the refrigerator.

Tip: Serve red fruit jelly as a pudding with vanilla custard or cream. As a sweet main meal, accompanied by milk, it will serve 4.

Accompaniment: To make **vanilla custard,** cut 1 vanilla pod open lengthways with the back of a knife and scrape out the pulp. Mix together 25 g/1 oz (3 tbsp) cornflour and 50 g/2 oz (¼ cup) sugar. Take 3 tbsp from the 500 ml/17 fl oz (2 cups) milk and stir into the cornflour-sugar mixture. Add the vanilla pulp to the rest of the milk and bring to the boil in a pan. Remove the pan from the heat and stir in the cornflour mixture with a whisk. Bring briefly to the boil again. Serve the sauce hot or leave to cool, stirring occasionally.

Sophisticated kugelhopf cake

Feiner Gugelhupf

Never change a winning cake

16 slices

For the yeast dough:

200 g/7 oz (⅞ cup) whipping cream
100 g/3 ½ oz (½ cup) butter or margarine
400 g/14 oz (3 ¼ cups) plain (all purpose) flour
1 sachet dried yeast
125 g/4 ½ oz (⅝ cup) sugar
1 sachet vanilla sugar
a few drops lemon extract
1 pinch salt
3 eggs (medium)
150 g/5 oz (¾ cup) raisins
100 g/3 ½ oz (⅔ cup) currants
100 g/3 ½ oz (⅞ cup) chopped almonds

Also:

a little icing (confectioners') sugar

Preparation time: 35 minutes, excl. rising time
Baking time: about 50 minutes

For each cake, the correct mould

1 For the dough, warm the cream in a small pan and melt the butter or margarine in it.

2 Mix the flour and dried yeast together thoroughly in a mixing bowl. Add the sugar, vanilla sugar, flavouring, salt, eggs and the warm cream-butter or margarine mixture. Mix the ingredients using a hand-mixer with dough hook attachment, first briefly on the lowest setting, then on the highest setting for about 5 minutes to make a smooth dough.

3 Briskly knead the raisins, currants and almonds into the dough. Put the dough in a warm place until it has doubled in size.

4 Preheat the oven.
Top/bottom heat: about 180 °C/350 °F (Gas mark 4)
Fan oven: about 160 °C/325 °F

5 Knead the dough briefly using a hand-mixer with dough hook attachment on the highest setting, put the dough in a kugelhopf mould (diameter 22 cm/9 in, greased) and put the dough again in a warm place to rise until it has doubled in size. Put the mould on a shelf in the bottom third of the preheated oven and bake for about 50 minutes.

6 Put the cake still in its tin on a wire rack and leave it to cool slightly. Then turn it out onto parchment paper on the rack and leave it to cool.

Variation: Instead of almonds, raisins and currants, you make the kugelhopf using 100 g/3 ½ oz (½ cup) finely chopped glacé cherries, 200 g/7 oz (1 ⅓ cups) dried, chopped apricots and 50 g/2 oz (⅓ cup) chopped pistachio nuts.

Sachertorte

A sweet celebrity from Austria with chocolate glaze and apricot jam

Horse-drawn carriages are the best way to discover the old city of Vienna

12 pieces

For the sponge:

150 g/5 oz dark chocolate (about 50% cocoa content)
6 egg whites (medium)
160 g/5 ½ oz (⅞ cup) butter or margarine (room temperature)
160 g/5 ½ oz (⅞ cup) sugar
1 sachet vanilla sugar
6 egg yolks (medium)
100 g/3 ½ oz (1 cup) breadcrumbs

For the filling:

125 g/4 ½ oz (½ cup) apricot jam

For the glaze:

60 g/2 oz (¼ cup) sugar
7 tbsp water
250 g/9 oz dark chocolate (about 50% cocoa content)

Preparation time: 45 minutes, excl. cooling time
Baking time: about 50 minutes

1 To make the sponge, first break the chocolate into small pieces. Melt two-thirds of them over low heat in a bain-marie (water bath), stirring until they melt. Remove the pan from the bain-marie, add the remaining chocolate and melt while stirring.

2 Preheat the oven.
Top/bottom heat: about 180 °C/350 °F (Gas mark 4)
Fan oven: about 160 °C/325 °F

3 Beat the egg white until stiff. Whisk the butter or margarine in a mixing bowl using a hand-mixer with whisk attachment at high speed until soft. Gradually add the sugar and vanilla sugar, whisking all the time until you obtain a smooth mixture.

4 Whisk in the egg yolks one after the other. Stir in the melted chocolate and breadcrumbs over medium heat. Very gently fold in the stiffly beaten egg whites. Now spoon the sponge mixture into a springform mould (diameter 26 cm/10 ¼ in, the bottom greased and lined with parchment paper). Put the mould on a shelf in the bottom third of the preheated oven. Bake for about 50 minutes.

5 Remove the cake from the tin and place on a cake rack lined with parchment paper. Leave to cool. Then remove the parchment paper and cut the cake horizontally once to make two layers. Place the bottom layer on a cake platter.

6 For the filling, spread the jam on the bottom layer, then put the top layer on top of it.

7 To make the glaze, add the sugar to the water in a pan and boil until it is completely dissolved. Remove the pan from the heat. Break 200 g/7 oz chocolate into pieces and stir in gradually; continue stirring until the chocolate has completely melted and the mixture is shiny.

8 Pour the glaze onto the middle of the cake and spread it evenly all over the cake by slightly "moving and tipping" it on the platter. If necessary, spread the glaze along the sides with a knife. To ensure that the glaze spreads evenly over the cake, lift the platter and "tap" it on a wooden surface once or twice.

9 Loosen the bottom of the cake from the cake platter by sliding a long knife under it; then slide the cake onto a cake stand by slightly tipping the cake platter and guiding the cake with the knife. Leave the icing to set.

10 To decorate the cake, melt the remaining chocolate in a bain-marie while stirring. Cut the cake into 12 slices. Pour the melted chocolate into a paper icing bag or a small freezer bag, cut off a small corner and write the word "Sacher" on each slice. Keep the cake in a cool place until serving.

Schwarzwälder Kirschtorte with alcohol

Taste this fabulous pleasure from the land of the cuckoo clock

12 pieces

For the fatless sponge:

3 eggs (medium)
100 g/3 ½ oz (½ cup) sugar
1 sachet vanilla sugar
80g/3 oz (generous ½ cup) plain (all purpose) flour
1 level tsp baking powder
25 g/1 oz (3 tbsp) cornflour (cornstarch)
10 g/⅓ oz (1 ½ tbsp) cocoa powder
a good pinch ground cinnamon

For the shortcrust pastry:

125 g/4 ½ oz (1 cup) plain (all purpose) flour
10 g/⅓ oz (1 ½ tbsp) cocoa powder
1 pinch baking powder
50 g/2 oz (¼ cup) sugar
1 sachet vanilla sugar
1 egg (medium)
50 g/2 oz (4 tbsp) butter or margarine (room temperature)

For the filling:

350 g/12 oz drained morello cherries (from the jar)
250 ml/8 fl oz (1 cup) cherry juice (from the jar)
30 g/1 oz (3 tbsp) cornflour (cornstarch)
about 25 g/1 oz (2 tbsp) sugar
about 3 tbsp Kirsch liqueur
1 sachet clear powdered gelatine
5 tbsp cold water
800 g/1 ¾ lb (3 ½ cups) chilled whipping cream
40 g/1 ½ oz (⅜ cup) sifted icing (confectioners') sugar
1 sachet vanilla sugar

For the decoration:

grated chocolate curls or grated chocolate

Preparation time: 75 minutes, excl. cooling time
Baking time: about 40 minutes

1 Preheat the oven.
Top/bottom heat: about 180 °C/350 °F (Gas mark 4)
Fan oven: about 160 °C/325 °F

2 For the sponge, put the eggs in a mixing bowl and whisk with a hand-mixer with whisk attachment on the highest setting for 1 minute until foamy. Mix together the sugar and vanilla sugar, sprinkle into the eggs while stirring for 1 minute, then whisk for 2 minutes more.

3 Mix the flour, baking powder, cocoa powder and cinnamon and whisk briefly on the lowest setting. Transfer the sponge mixture into a springform mould (diameter 26 cm/10 ¼ in, the bottom greased and lines with parchment paper) and smooth the surface. Put the mould on a shelf in the bottom third of the oven. Bake for about 25 minutes.

4 Take the sponge cake out of the mould and put on a cake rack lined with parchment paper. Leave to cool.

5 For the shortcrust pastry, mix the flour, cocoa powder and baking powder in a bowl. Add all the other ingredients and mix using a hand-mixer with dough hook attachment, first briefly on the lowest setting, then on the highest setting until the shortcrust pastry has the right texture. Then shape into a ball with your hands. Roll out the pastry on the bottom of the springform mould (diameter 26 cm/10 ¼ in, greased) and prick several times with a fork. Put the ring back on the mould.

6 Put the mould on a shelf in the bottom third of the oven and bake the shortcrust pastry base at the same oven temperature as the sponge for about 15 minutes.

7 Loosen the shortcrust pastry from the bottom of the mould as soon as it comes out of the oven but leave it on the bottom of the mould to cool on a cake rack. Peel the parchment paper off the sponge and cut once horizontally into two layers.

8 To make the filling, drain the cherries thoroughly and reserve the juice. Pour off 250 ml/8 fl oz (1 cup) and put to one side. Reserve 12 cherries to decorate the cake and put them on kitchen paper.

9 Mix together the cornflour (cornstarch) and sugar, add 4 tbsp of the cherry juice and stir well. Bring the rest of the juice to the boil. Take off the heat and stir in the cornflour, sugar and juice mixture. Bring to the boil again, stir in the cherries and leave to cool. Add the Kirsch liqueur.

10 Add the gelatine to water in a small pan and stir; leave to soak for 5 minutes and heat up, stirring all the time, until the gelatine has dissolved completely. Whip the cream almost stiff. First stir about 2 tbsp of whipped cream into the dissolved gelatine, then whisk the gelatine mixture immediately into the whipped cream and whisk until stiff. Mix together the icing (confectioners') sugar and vanilla sugar and stir into the cream-gelatine mixture.

11 Put the shortcrust pastry base on a cake platter. Spread the cherry mixture on top, leaving a an edge 1 cm/⅜ in wide free all round. Spread one-third of the whipped cream mixture on top. Now put the bottom sponge layer on top and spread half the remaining whipped cream mixture over it. Next put the top layer on it and press down lightly. Put 3 tbsp of the whipped cream mixture in a piping bag with a star-shaped nozzle and put to one side. Spread the rest of the mixture on the top and sides of the cake to cover it completely. Decorate with piped whipped cream and garnish with the reserved chocolate flakes and cherries. Leave the cake in the refrigerator for at least two hours.

Frankfurt crown

Frankfurter Kranz

Definitely the king of any Sunday afternoon

16 slices

For the sponge:
100 g/3 ½ oz (½ cup) butter or margarine (room temperature)
150 g/5 oz (¾ cup) sugar
1 sachet vanilla sugar
4 drops Dr. Oetker Natural Lemon Extract
1 pinch salt
3 eggs (medium)
150 g/6 oz (scant 1 ¼ cups) plain (all purpose) flour
50 g/2 oz (6 tbsp) cornflour (cornstarch)
2 level tsp baking powder

For the almond praline:
10 g/⅓ oz (2 tsp) butter
60 g/2 oz (¼ cup) sugar
125 g/4 ½ oz (1 ½ cups) peeled chopped almonds

For the butter cream:
40 g/1 ½ oz (5 tbsp) custard powder (vanilla pudding mix)
100 g/3 ½ oz (½ cup) sugar
500 ml/17 fl oz (2 cups) milk
250 g/9 oz (1 ¼ cups) butter (room temperature)

Also:
3 tbsp red currant jelly or strawberry jam
some glacé cherries

Preparation time: 60 minutes, excl. cooling time
Baking time: about 40 minutes

1 Preheat the oven.
Top/bottom heat: about 180 °C/350 °F (Gas mark 4)
Fan oven: about 160 °C/325 °F

2 To make the sponge, whisk the butter or margarine using a hand-mixer with whisk attachment at the highest setting until soft. Mix in the sugar, vanilla sugar, lemon extract and salt little by little. Continue until you have a smooth mixture.

3 Whisk in the eggs, one after the other, for ½ minute each. Mix the flour, cornflour and baking powder and in two stages whisk into the egg and sugar mixture on the medium setting. Spoon into a ring mould (diameter 22 cm/9 in, greased) and smooth the surface. Put on a shelf in the bottom third of the preheated oven. Bake for about 40 minutes.

4 Remove from the oven and leave the cake in the mould for about 10 minutes. Then take it out and put it on parchment paper on a wire rack to cool.

5 For the praline, heat the butter, sugar and almond in a pan until the mixture has turned brown. Pour onto piece of foil and leave to cool.

6 For the butter cream, make custard following the instructions on the packet but with 100 g/3 ½ oz (½ cup) sugar and with milk. Leave the custard to cool (but do not refrigerate), stirring occasionally.

7 Whisk the butter using a hand-held mixer with whisk attachment until soft. Then stir in the cooled custard, spoonful by spoonful, having made sure that the butter and custard are at room temperature (the butter cream might curdle otherwise).

8 Cut the ring horizontally twice to make three layers. Stir the jelly with a whisk until smooth or rub the jam through a sieve and spread on the bottom layer. Now spread half the butter cream on the bottom two layers. Then put all the layers back on top of each other to reconstruct the ring.

9 Coat the entire ring inside and out with the rest of the butter cream (having first put 1–2 tbsp aside) and sprinkle with the praline. Put the reserved butter cream in a piping bag fitted with a star-shaped nozzle and decorate the top of the ring with it, then garnish with glacé cherries. Put the cake in the refrigerator for about 2 hours.

Cheese and cream cake

Käse-Sahne-Torte

What could be better with a nice cup of coffee

12 pieces

For the sponge:

150g/5 oz (⅔ cup) butter or margarine (room temperature)
150g/5 oz (⅔ cup) sugar
1 sachet vanilla sugar
1 pinch salt
3 eggs (medium)
150 g/6 oz (scant 1 ¼ cups) plain (all purpose) flour
1 level tsp baking powder

For the filling:

8 sheets white gelatine
750 g/1 lb 10 oz low fat quark
150g/5 oz (⅔ cup) sugar
1 sachet vanilla sugar
100 ml/3 ½ fl oz (⅜ cup) lemon juice
1 tsp grated lemon zest
400 g/14 oz whipping cream (min. 30% fat)

For sprinkling:

some icing (confectioners') sugar

Preparation time: 45 minutes, excl. cooling time
Baking time: 25–30 minutes

1 Preheat the oven:
Top/bottom heat: about 200 °C/400 °F (Gas mark 6)
Fan oven: about 180 °C/350 °F

2 To make the sponge, mix the butter or margarine with a hand-held mixer on the highest setting until soft. Gradually stir in the sugar, vanilla sugar and salt. Continue stirring until the mixture has become smooth and even.

3 Stir in the eggs one by one (stir for about ½ minute per egg). Mix together the flour and baking powder and stir into the mixture briefly on the medium setting.

4 Transfer the sponge into a springform mould (diameter 26 cm/9 ½ in with greased bottom) and smooth the surface to make it even. Put the mould on the middle shelf in the preheated oven. Bake the cake for 25–30 minutes.

5 Place the springform mould on a wire rack and let the cake cool slightly; then carefully remove it from the mould and leave to cool on a wire rack lined with baking paper.

6 Cut the cake base in half horizontally with a serrated knife. Place the lower half on a cake plate. Place a cake ring round it, or use the ring of the springform mould, having first washed it.

7 For the filling, soak the gelatine following the instructions on the packet. Mix together the quark, sugar, vanilla sugar, lemon juice and lemon zest until the mixture is smooth and even. Whip the cream until stiff.

8 Squeeze the gelatine lightly and dissolve in a small pan over low heat, stirring all the time. Stir 4 tbsp of the quark mixture into the dissolved gelatine, then add this to the rest of the quark mixture. Stir the cream into the mixture. Spoon the quark-cream mixture on the lower base and make it even.

9 Cut the upper layer of the cake into 12 slices. Place these on the filling and press down lightly. Cover and keep in the refrigerator for at least 3 hours before serving. Carefully loosen and remove the ring. Sprinkle with icing (confectioner's) sugar before serving.

The medieval city centre of Linz

Linzer Torte

The legendary raspberry jam speciality from the capital of Upper Austria

12 pieces

For the shortcrust pastry:

200 g/7 oz (scant 1 ¾ cups) plain (all purpose) flour
1 level tsp baking powder
100 g/3 ½ oz (½ cup) sugar
1 sachet vanilla sugar
1 pinch ground cloves
1 level tsp ground cinnamon
1 egg (medium)
1 egg white (medium)
100 g/3 ½ oz (½ cup) butter or margarine (room temperature)
100 g/3 ½ oz (1 cup) ground almonds

For the topping:

100 g/3 ½ oz (⅜ cup) raspberry jam

For coating:

1 egg yolk (medium)
1 tsp milk

Preparation time: 30 minutes, excl. cooling time
Baking time: about 30 minutes

1 To make the shortcrust pastry, mix together the flour and baking powder in a mixing bowl. Add all the other ingredients for the shortcrust pastry and whisk everything with a hand-mixer with dough hook attachment, first on the lowest setting, then on the highest setting until all the ingredients have been incorporated and formed a shortcrust pastry. Then shape into a roll with your hands. Wrap the pastry in clingfilm (plastic film) and put in the refrigerator for about 30 minutes.

2 Preheat the oven:
Top/bottom heat: about 180 °C/350 °F (Gas mark 4)
Fan oven: about 160 °C/325 °F

3 Roll out half the pastry to form a circle the same size as the base of a springform mould (diameter 26 cm/10 ¼ in) and cut out 16–20 strips using a pastry wheel. Roll out the rest of the pastry on the base of the springform mould (greased) and put the side back on.

4 For the topping, spread the jam on the pastry base, leaving an edge about 1 cm/⅜ wide free of jam all round. Arrange the strips of pastry on top to form a trellis pattern. Whisk together the egg yolk and milk and brush over the strips of pastry.

5 Put the mould in the bottom third of the preheated oven and bake for about 30 minutes.

6 Remove the torte from the oven, carefully release the side of the springform mould and remove it. Then lift the torte off the mould base and leave to cool on a cake rack.

Variation: To make **Linzer slices,** double the quantities. Roll out half the pastry the same size as the baking sheet and cut into strips. Roll out the rest of the pastry on a greased baking sheet (30 x 40 cm/12 x 16 in). Spread the jam on the pastry base and arrange the strips to form a trellis pattern. Bake the cake as described in the recipe. When cold, cut into slices of the size of your choice.

Friesische Streuseltorte

A delicious indulgence for any occasion

12 pieces
For the shortcrust pastry:
250 g/9 oz (2 cups) plain (all purpose) flour
1 pinch baking powder
2 sachets vanilla sugar
150 g/5 oz crème fraîche
175 g/6 oz (⅞ cup) butter or margarine
(room temperature)

For the crumble:
150 g/6 oz (scant 1 ¼ cups) plain (all purpose) flour
75 g/3 oz (⅓ cup) sugar
1 sachet vanilla sugar
1 pinch ground cinnamon
100 g/3 ½ oz (½ cup) butter (room temperature)

For the filling:
500 g/18 oz (2 ¼ cups) chilled whipping cream
(min. 30 % fat)
25 g/1 oz (2 tbsp) sugar
1 sachet vanilla sugar
450 g/1 lb plum butter

Preparation time: 50 minutes, excl. cooling time
Baking time: about 15 minutes per layer

1 Preheat the oven.
Top/bottom heat: about 200 °C/400 °F (Gas mark 6)
Fan oven: about 180 °C/350 °F

2 To make the shortcrust pastry, mix together the flour and baking powder in a mixing bowl. Add all the other ingredients for the shortcrust pastry and whisk everything using a hand-mixer with dough hook attachment, first on the lowest setting, then on the highest setting. Then knead briefly on a lightly-floured work surface.

3 Divide the pastry into 4 portions of equal size and shape into balls. Roll out one portion on the bottom of a springform mould (diameter 26 cm/10 ¼ in, greased), prick several times with a fork and put the side of the springform mould back on.

4 To make the crumble, mix together the flour, vanilla sugar and cinnamon in a mixing bowl. Add the butter and mix everything using a hand-mixer with whisk attachment to make the crumble of the desired texture.

5 Spread one quarter of the crumble evenly over the pastry base. Put the springform mould in the bottom third of the preheated oven and bake the base for about 15 minutes. Prepare the other three layers in the same way and bake.

6 When baked, remove the pastry bases immediately from the springform mould and leave to cool separately on a cake rack. Cut one of the layers into 12 slices while it is still warm.

7 For the filling, whisk the whipping cream with the sugar and vanilla sugar until stiff and put in portions in a pastry bag with a star-shaped nozzle (diameter about 8 mm/⅓ in). Spread a third of the plum compote on each of the three uncut layers, then pipe onto each one a third of the whipped cream. Place the layers on top of each, ending with the layers already cut into slices, to make a tart. Put the tart in the refrigerator for about 1 hour. Sprinkle with icing (confectioners') sugar before serving if you like.

Tip: It is best to cut the tart with a serrated knife.

Sand, waves and a light breeze.
Here you can really relax.

At the end of June they are ripe! Now the red currant harvest can begin.

Träublestorte

Red currant meringue cake

This will make a lazy summer afternoon perfect

12 pieces

For the shortcrust pastry:
250 g/9 oz (2 cups) plain (all purpose) flour
65 g/2 ¼ oz (scant ⅓ cup) sugar
1 sachet vanilla sugar
1 pinch salt
1 egg (medium)
125 g/4 ½ oz (⅝ cup) butter or margarine (room temperature)

Also:
1 tbsp plain (all purpose) flour

For the topping:
500 g/18 oz red currants
5 egg whites (medium)
175 g/6 oz (⅞ cup) sugar
100 g/3 ½ oz (1 cup) ground almonds
60 g/2 oz (6 tbsp) cornflour (cornstarch)

Preparation time: 45 minutes
Baking time: about 72 minutes

1 Preheat the oven.
Top/bottom heat: about 200 °C/400 °F (Gas mark 6)
Fan oven: about 180 °C/350 °F

2 Put all the ingredients for the shortcrust pastry in a mixing bowl. Whisk everything using a hand-mixer with dough hook attachment, first on the lowest setting, then on the highest setting until all the ingredients have been incorporated and formed a shortcrust pastry. Then shape into a roll with your hands.

3 Roll out two-thirds of the shortcrust pastry on the base of a springform mould (diameter 26 cm/10 ¼ in, greased). Then put the side of the mould round it again.

4 Knead 1 tbsp flour into the rest of the dough and shape into a long roll. Place the roll along the edge of the pastry base and press it against the sides of the springform mould to make an edge about 4 cm/1 ½ in high. Prick the base several times with a fork.

5 Put the springform mould on the bottom shelf in the preheated oven. Blind-bake for about 12 minutes.

6 For the topping, rinse the red currants, leave to drain and pull the red currants off the sprigs. Beat the egg so stiff that if you make an incision with a knife, the cut remains visible. Gradually whisk in the sugar. Carefully fold in the almonds and cornflour (cornstarch), then fold in the red currants.

7 Reduce the oven temperature by 20 °C/25 °F so that top/bottom heat is about 180 °C/350 °F (Gas mark 4) or fan oven: about 160 °C/325 °F. Spoon the red currant-meringue mixture on the still hot pastry base to form a dome. Put the springform mould back in the oven and bake the cake for another 60 minutes (the meringue mixture should be golden brown).

8 Leave the cake in the springform mould and place it on a cake rack to cool for 1–2 hours, then remove carefully from the mould.

Eierschecke

Egg-custard cake

Originally from Saxony, three layers make this a star of the cake universe

The historic panorama of Dresden, known as 'Florence on the Elbe' with the Frauenkirche and the White Fleet of paddle steamers

20 pieces

For the pastry base:

125 ml/4 fl oz (½ cup) milk
100 g/3 ½ oz (½ cup) butter or margarine
300 g/12 oz (2 ½ cups) plain (all purpose) flour
1 sachet dried yeast
50 g/2 oz (¼ cup) sugar
1 sachet vanilla sugar
4 drops lemon extract
1 pinch salt
1 egg (medium)

For the quark filling:

40 g/1 ½ oz (5 tbsp) custard powder (vanilla pudding mix)
40 g/1 ½ oz (scant ¼ cup) sugar
500 ml/17 fl oz (2 cups) milk
500 g/18 oz low fat quark
50 g/2 oz (scant ½ cup) raisins or currants

For the egg cream:

4 egg whites (medium)
125 g/4 ½ oz (generous ½ cup) butter (room temperature)
125 g/4 ½ oz (generous ½ cup) sugar
4 egg yolks (medium)
15 g/ ½ oz (2 tbsp) cornflour (cornstarch)

Preparation time: 40 minutes, excl. rising time
Baking time: about 30 minutes

1 To make the pastry, heat the milk in a small pan. Melt the butter or margarine in it.

2 Put the flour in a mixing bowl and add the dry yeast, mixing thoroughly. Add the sugar, vanilla sugar, flavouring, salt, the egg and the warm milk and butter or margarine mixture. Mix together all the ingredients with a mixer (kneading hook), first briefly on the lowest setting, then on the highest setting for about 5 minutes to obtain a smooth, even dough. Cover and place in a warm place until it has visibly increased in volume.

3 For the quark filling, cook the vanilla pudding powder, sugar and milk, following the instructions on the packet. Put in a bowl and place some clingfilm (plastic wrap) directly on the surface of the filling and refrigerate.

4 Preheat the oven:
Top/bottom heat: about 200 °C/400 °F (Gas mark 6)
Fan oven: about 180 °C/350 °F

5 Stir the quark and raisins into the cooled custard. Knead the pastry again briefly on a lightly floured surface, roll up into cylinder and then roll out onto a high-sided baking pan (30 x 40 cm/12 x 16 in, greased). Spread the quark filling on top.

6 For the egg cream, beat the egg whites until they form stiff peaks. Mix the butter with the hand-held mixer until it has softened sufficiently. Now stir in the sugar little by little

and continue stirring until you have obtained a smooth, even mass. Stir in the egg yolks one by one.

7 Put the beaten egg whites on top of the egg yolk mixture, then sprinkle with the cornflour (cornstarch) and very carefully fold the two mixtures into each other. Spread the egg and cream over the quark mixture and smooth to make it even.

8 Put the baking pan on a shelf in the bottom third of the oven. Bake for about 30 minutes.

9 Place the baking tin on a wire rack and leave the cake to cool.

Tips: Before incorporating the raisins into the quark mixture, soak them in 2 tbsp of rum.
If you do not have a baking pan with high sides, you can make the cake in a roasting pan (30 x 40 cm/12 x 16 in) or use a baking frame the same size as the baking pan on top of a flat baking sheet.

Danube waves cake

Donauwellen

Ride the waves with this delicious pleasure

River cruises on the Danube are a relaxing pleasure

20 pieces

For the sponge:

250 g/9 oz (1 cup) butter or margarine (room temperature)
200 g/7 oz sugar
1 sachet vanilla sugar
1 pinch salt
5 eggs (medium)
175 g/6 oz (scant 1 ½ cups) plain (all purpose) flour
3 level tsp baking powder
20 g/ ¾ oz (4 tbsp) sieved cocoa powder
1 tbsp milk

700 g/1 lb 8 oz drained sour cherries (from the jar)

For the butter cream:

40 g/1 ½ oz (5 tbsp) custard powder (vanilla pudding mix)
100 g/3 ½ oz (½ cup) sugar
500 ml/17 fl oz (2 cups) milk
250 g/9 oz (1 cup) butter or margarine (room temperature)

For the glaze:

200 g/7 oz dark chocolate (about 50 % cocoa content)
2 tbsp cooking oil, e. g. sunflower oil

Preparation time: 45 minutes, excl. cooling time
Baking time: about 40 minutes

1 Preheat the oven:
Top/bottom heat: about 200 °C/400 °F (Gas mark 6)
Fan oven: about 180 °C/350 °F

2 To make the sponge, mix the butter or margarine with a hand-held mixer on the highest setting until sufficiently softened. Gradually stir in the sugar, vanilla sugar and salt. Continue stirring until the mixture has acquired a smooth, homogenous consistency.

3 Stir in the eggs one by one (stir about ½ minute for each egg). Mix together the flour and baking powder and stir in two portions with the mixer set on a medium setting. Spread two-thirds of the dough on a greased high-sided baking pan (30 x 40 cm/12 x 16 in). Stir the cocoa powder together with the milk into the rest of the dough. Now spread the dark-coloured dough evenly over the light-coloured dough.

4 Place the sour cherries briefly on kitchen paper towel, then distribute across the dark-coloured dough and press them slightly into the dough with the back of a spoon. Place the baking pan in the preheated oven (bottom third). Bake the base for about 40 minutes.

5 Now place the baking pan on a cake rack to cool.

6 To make the butter cream, prepare a custard with the vanilla pudding powder, 100 g/3 ½ oz (½ cup) sugar and milk, following the instructions on the packet. Allow the custard to cool (but do not put in the refrigerator), stirring occasionally.

7 Mix the butter with a hand-held mixer until sufficiently softened. Now spoon the cooled custard into the softened butter, making sure that the butter and custard are both at room temperature because otherwise the butter cream may curdle. Now spread the butter cream on the cooled pastry base. Cover the cake and put in the refrigerator for about 1 hour.

8 To make the chocolate icing, break the chocolate into pieces and melt with the oil in a bain-marie (water bath) over low heat, stirring all the time. Pour the chocolate icing on the set butter cream and decorate with a cake comb.

Tips: When cooling the custard, place clingfilm (plastic wrap) directly on the surface. This will prevent a skin from forming on top and the custard will not need stirring while cooling.
This cake is suitable for freezing.
If you do not have a baking pan with high sides, you can use a baking frame the same size as the baking pan placed on a flat baking-sheet and prepare the cake as described in the recipe.

Wiener Apfelstrudel

Viennese apple strudel

Smells wonderful, tastes wonderful

12 slices

For the strudel pastry:
200 g/7 oz (scant 1 ¾ cups cups)
plain (all purpose) flour
1 pinch salt
75 ml/3 fl oz (⅜ cup) lukewarm water
50 g/2 oz (4 tbsp) melted butter or margarine or 3 tbsp cooking oil, e. g. sunflower oil

50 g/2 oz (¾ cup) breadcrumbs

For the filling:
1–1.5 kg/3 ¼ lb apples, e. g. Cox's Orange, Elstar
3 drops lemon extract
75 g/3 oz (⅜ cup) butter or margarine
50 g/2 oz (⅓ cup) raisins
100 g/3 ½ oz (½ cup) sugar
1 sachet vanilla sugar
50 g/2 oz (⅜ cup) peeled ground
or chopped almonds

Preparation time: 50 minutes, excl. standing time
Baking time: about 50 minutes

1 For the pastry, put the flour in a mixing bowl. Add all the other ingredients and mix using a hand-mixer with dough hook attachment, first briefly on the lowest setting, then on the highest setting to make a smooth dough. Boil the water in a small pan, pour the water away and dry the pan.

2 Place the dough on parchment paper in the hot pan. Cover the pan with a lid and leave the dough to rise for about 30 minutes. Put the breadcrumbs in a pan without oil until golden brown and turn onto a plate.

3 Preheat the oven.
Top/bottom heat: about 180 °C/350 °F (Gas mark 4)
Fan oven: about 160 °C/325 °F

4 For the filling, peel the apples, cut into quarters, core and cut into thin sticks. Stir in the lemon essence. Melt the butter or margarine. Cut the dough in half and roll out each half on a large floured tea towel.

5 Spread a little fat on the rolled-out dough, then pull to make a rectangle (about 35 x 25 cm/14 x 10 in). Cut off the edges if they are too thick. Spread two-thirds of the fat on the rolled-out sheet of dough and sprinkle the breadcrumbs on top (leave an edge about 2 cm/¾ in wide uncovered all round).

6 Sprinkle the apple sticks, raisins, sugar, vanilla sugar and almonds one after the other on the dough. Fold the uncovered edges of the short sides over the filling. Using the cloth to help you, roll up the dough, covered with filling, starting from the long side and press the ends together firmly.

7 Place the strudel on a baking sheet (greased) with the seam downwards and spread a little fat over the top. Put the baking sheet in the bottom third of the preheated oven and bake for about 50 minutes.

8 After about 30 minutes spread the rest of the fat over the strudel.

9 When the strudel is done, take it out of the oven and leave to cool on the baking sheet placed on a cake rack or serve warm.

Tips: Add a touch of sophistication to the filling by adding a few drops of rum flavouring.

The Palm House in Vienna's Burggarten is a popular meeting place

Cold dog cake

Kalter Hund

Completely energy-efficent: a cake without baking

20 slices

For the chocolate cream:
150 g/5 oz dark coating chocolate (about 50% cocoa ontent)
450 g/1 lb full milk coating chocolate (about 30% cocoa content)
150 ml/5 fl oz (5⁄8 cup) coconut oil
200 g/7 oz (7⁄8 cup) whipping cream
2 sachets vanilla sugar

Also:
about 300 g/12 oz petit beurre biscuits (butter cookies)

1 large freezer bag

Preparation time: 60 minutes, excl. cooling time

1 Cut open a freezer bag and line a rectangular tin (25 x 11 cm/10 x 4 ½ in) with it.

2 To make the chocolate filling, chop the two kinds of coating chocolate into pieces. Heat the cream in a pan. Add the coconut oil and the chopped chocolate and let it melt in the hot cream, stirring all the time. Now stir in the vanilla sugar.

3 Now line the bottom of the baking tin with a layer of petit beurre biscuits; if necessary cut the biscuits with a serrated knife or break them to make them fit. Spoon enough chocolate filling on the biscuits to cover them. Continue in this way, alternating a layer of biscuits and a layer of chocolate filling to fill the tin (7–8 layers).

4 Put the tin in the refrigerator for about 5 hours (overnight is even better) to set the chocolate filling.

5 Very carefully turn put the contents onto a rectangular platter and gently pull the freezer bag away. Keep the pudding in the refrigerator until you are ready to serve it.

Tips: Stir 2 single-cup sachets (2 g each) of instant espresso coffee into the chocolate filling.
To ensure that the freezer bag lining the tin does not slide about, grease the tin lightly before lining the tin with the freezer bag.

Cold dog with a difference.

Hazelnut triangles

Nussecken

You'll like these even if geometry is not your strong point

30 pieces

For the shortcrust pastry:
225 g/8 oz (2 ¼ cups) plain (all purpose) flour
1 level tsp baking powder
100 g/3 ½ oz (½ cup) sugar
1 sachet vanilla sugar
1 egg (medium)
1 tbsp water
100 g/3 ½ oz (½ cup) butter or margarine (room temperature)

For the topping:
150 g/5 oz (¾ cup) butter
150 g/5 oz (¾ cup) sugar
2 sachets vanilla sugar
3 tbsp water
100 g/3 ½ oz (1 cup) ground hazelnuts
200 g/7 oz (2 ½ cups) chopped hazelnuts
3 tbsp apricot jam

100 g/3 ½ oz dark chocolate (about 50 % cocoa content)

Preparation time: 30 minutes, excl. cooling time
Baking time: about 25 minutes
Keeping time: about 3 weeks in an airtight container

1 Preheat the oven.
Top/bottom heat: about 180 °C/350 °F (Gas mark 4)
Fan oven: about 160 °C/325 °F

2 To make the shortcrust pastry, mix together the flour and baking powder in a mixing bowl. Add all the other ingredients for the shortcrust pastry and whisk everything using a hand-mixer with dough hook attachment, first on the lowest setting, then on the highest setting.

3 Knead briefly on a floured work surface. Then shape into a roll with your hands.

4 For the topping, warm and melt the butter, sugar, vanilla sugar and water gently in a pan, stirring all the time. Stir in the ground and chopped hazelnuts. Remove the pan from the heat and leave the topping to cool for about 10 minutes.

5 Roll out the pastry on a baking sheet (30 x 40 cm/ 12 x 16 in, greased). Spread the apricot jam over the rolled-out pastry, then spread the topping evenly over the jam. Put the baking sheet on the middle shelf in the preheated oven and bake for about 25 minutes.

6 Put the baking sheet with the baked pastry on a cake rack and leave to cool for about 20 minutes. Then cut into squares of about 8 x 8 cm/3 x 3 in and cut each square diagonally to make triangles.

7 To make the glaze, break the chocolate into pieces. Melt two-thirds of them in a bain-marie over low heat, stirring all the time. Remove the pan from the heat and add the remaining chocolate, stirring while it melts. Dip the two pointed corners of the triangles in the chocolate. Put the triangles on a cake rack or parchment paper and allow the glaze to set.

Tips: Instead of just dipping the two pointed corners in the melted chocolate, you can cover the whole triangle with melted chocolate. This will save time since it will be much quicker.
To make smaller nut triangles (about 140 biscuits), cut the sheet of baked pastry into small squares of about 4 x 4 cm/ 1 ½ x 1 ½ in, then cut them in half diagonally.

Variation: To make **coconut triangles,** replace the hazelnuts with 200 g/7 oz (⅞ cup) grated coconut.

Wintertime and the Christmas market in Annaberg-Buchholz, Erzgebirge

Vanilla crescent cookies

Vanillekipferl

Austrian Christmas cookies that instantly melt in the mouth

60 pieces

For the shortcrust pastry:

200 g/7 oz plain (all purpose) flour
1 pinch baking powder
100 g/3½ oz (½ cup) sugar
1 sachet vanilla sugar
2 egg yolks (medium)
170 g/6 oz (¾ cup) butter or margarine
100 g/3½ oz (1 cup) ground almonds

For sprinkling:

50 g/2 oz (1 cup) icing (confectioners') sugar
1 sachet vanilla sugar

Preparation time: 70 minutes, excl. cooling time
Baking time: about 10 minutes each baking sheet
Keeping time: about 3 weeks in a well-sealed container

1 To make the dough, mix together the flour and baking powder in a mixing bowl. Add the rest of the ingredients and stir with a mixer (kneading hook), at first briefly on the lowest setting, then on the highest setting until all the ingredients are completely incorporated. Then knead the mixture on a lightly floured work surface to make a dough. Divide the dough into two portions. Wrap each portion in clingfilm (plastic wrap) and place in the refrigerator for a while.

2 Preheat the oven:
Top/bottom heat: about 180 °C/350 °F (Gas mark 4)
Fan oven: about 160 °C/325 °F

3 Shape one portion of the dough into finger-thick cylinders and cut into pieces 6 cm/2½ in long. Make the pieces slightly thinner at the ends. Arrange the pieces individually on a baking sheet (greased and lined with parchment paper) and shape into crescents.

4 Work the second portion of dough in the same way. Put the baking sheets in the preheated oven one after the other. If you have a fan oven, you can bake them together. Bake the crescent cookies for about 10 minutes (per baking sheet).

5 Mix together the icing (confectioner's) sugar and vanilla sugar in a small bowl.

6 Slide the cookies and the parchment paper underneath them onto a wire rack. While they are still warm sprinkle with the sugar mixture and allow to cool.

Berliner with alcohol

Doughnuts

Traditional doughnuts – one of the nicest ways to eat jam

14–16 pieces

For the yeast dough:

125 ml/4 fl oz (½ cup) milk
100 g/3½ oz (½ cup) butter or margarine
500 g/18 oz (4 cups) plain (all purpose) flour
1 sachet dried yeast
30 g/1 oz (3 tbsp) sugar
1 sachet vanilla sugar
1 tbsp rum
1 level tsp salt
2 eggs (medium)
1 egg yolk (medium)

For the deep-frier:

deep-frying oil

For the filling:

300 g/10 oz (1 cup) jam of your choice
or 250 g/9 oz (1 cup) plum butter or jelly

For the coating:

a little sugar

Preparation and baking time: about 60 minutes, excl. rising time

1 To make the dough, heat the milk in a small pan, add the butter or margarine and melt it in the hot milk.

2 Mix the flour and dried yeast carefully together in a mixing bowl. Add all the other ingredients, the warm milk and fat mixture and mix everything using a hand-mixer with dough hook attachment, first briefly on the lowest setting, then on the highest setting for about 5 minutes until you have a smooth dough. Cover the dough and put in a warm place to rise until it has visibly increased in volume.

3 Sprinkle a little flour over the dough and knead again briefly on the work surface. Now roll out the dough onto the lightly floured work surface until it is about 1 cm/⅜ in thick and cut out about 14–16 circles with a diameter of about 7 cm/2¾ in. Now put the circles between two floured tea towels to rise until they have visibly increased in volume.

4 Meanwhile put the oil or fat in a chip pan or saucepan and heat to 175 °C/350 °F so that it forms small bubbles when you put the handle of a wooden spoon in it.

5 Put the doughnuts in the hot fat in instalments and deep-fry until golden brown on both sides. Then lift them out of the fat with a skimming ladle and leave to drain on kitchen paper.

6 To make the filling, rub the jam through a sieve or stir the plum butter or jelly until smooth. Then put in a piping bag with long, thin nozzle. Stick the nozzle into the light-coloured band on the side of the doughnut and pipe in some filling.

7 Coat the doughnuts in sugar when still warm and leave to cool on a cake rack.

Tips: In step 3 you can alternatively divide the dough into 14–16 portions of similar size and then shape these into balls.
To make **doughnuts with a sugar glaze,** dilute icing (confectioners') sugar with sufficient water to make a spreadable glaze. Spread this on the top of each doughnut.

New Year's Eve and Carnival are times for masses of doughnuts

General information

Please read the complete recipe before starting to cook, or better still, before buying the ingredients. This often makes the individual steps and the way they relate to each other clearer.

List of ingredients

The ingredients are listed in the order in which they are used.

Steps

The recipes are divided into steps, in the order in which they were tested.

Preparation and cooking times

The preparation time is a guide to the time taken to prepare the dish. Longer periods without activity, such as refrigeration, cooling, thawing and marinating times, are not included. Cooking and baking times are given separately in the recipe instructions.

Oven settings and baking and cooking times

The temperatures, baking times and cooking times given in the recipes are approximate and may be greater or less depending on the particular heating capacity of your oven. After the specified cooking time has elapsed, check that the dish is fully cooked.
It is useful to have an oven thermometer to check the oven temperature at a glance.

Shelf height

For tall-sided pans and other large items, the shelf is usually in the bottom position in the oven, while for shallow or small dishes the shelf is normally in the middle position. Cakes, biscuits and pastries are best baked in the middle of the oven. Variations are possible depending on the design of your oven. Check the maker's recommendations.

Measurements

The measurements used in the recipes are metric (grams, kilograms, litres, millilitres, centimetres and millimetres), with equivalents given in the US customary system of pounds, ounces, fluid ounces and inches. Where appropriate, volume measurements have also been supplied, in teaspoons, tablespoons and cups. To avoid clumsy fractions, the equivalents are not exact, but they will work just as well. The recipes were tested using metric quantities.
Where the measurement is "scant", measure level, then remove 2 tablespoons. Where it is "generous", add 2 tablespoons.

Flour measurements

The weight of a cup of flour will vary depending on how it is filled. In these recipes, one cup of plain (all purpose) flour is equivalent to 125 g/4½ oz. To achieve this, the flour in its bag or container should be stirred lightly with a scoop, then it is scooped into the cup measure and levelled off flat across the top.
Using the cup measure to scoop the flour directly from the container will end up with flour that is more densely packed, weighing up to one-third more than is specified in the recipe. Filling a cup measure with sifted flour will end up with less flour than that used in the recipe.
For greatest accuracy, it is best to use a scale.

Abbreviations

tbsp	=	tablespoon
tsp	=	teaspoon
g	=	gram
kg	=	kg
ml	=	millilitre
oz	=	ounce
fl oz	=	fluid ounce
lb	=	pound
°C	=	degrees Celsius
°F	=	degrees Fahrenheit
excl.	=	excluding

Pork with crackling

Krustenbraten

Front cover recipe

6 servings
salt water
1.25 kg/2 lb 12 oz pork leg with skin
2 onions
1 bunch soup vegetables (carrot, celeriac, leek)
20 g/¾ oz (1 ½ tbsp) butter or margarine
500 ml/17 fl oz (2 cups) beer
salt
freshly ground black pepper
1 tsp ground caraway seeds
6 cloves
a little broth or water if needed
1 tbsp cornflour (cornstarch)

Preparation time: 2 hours

1 Bring plenty of salted water to the boil in a large pan. Simmer the pork on a low heat for about 45 minutes.

2 Meanwhile, peel and quarter the onions. Rinse, clean and drain the vegetables, then cut into small pieces. Heat the butter or margarine in a roasting pan and fry the vegetables well. Then pour in half the beer.

3 Preheat the oven:
Top/bottom heat: 200– 220 °C/400–425 °F (Gas mark 6–7)
Fan oven: 180 –200°C/350–400 °F

4 Remove the meat from the pan and drain. Cut crisscross incisions in the skin about 1 cm/⅜ in deep. Sprinkle with salt, pepper and caraway. Push the cloves into points where the incisions cross.

5 Place the meat on the vegetables in the roasting pan. Put the roasting pan in a preheated oven. Cook the roast for about 45 minutes. From time to time pour some beer over the meat. 10 minutes before the end of cooking time, brush the meat with beer. If there is not enough liquid, add a little stock or water.

6 Remove the meat, cover and leave to rest for a few minutes. Pour the cooking residue through a sieve into a small pan and bring to a boil. Mix cornflour (cornstarch) with a little water and stir. Cook the sauce for about 5 minutes, stirring from time to time, then season with salt and pepper.

Accompaniment: Savoy cabbage and potato dumplings or thick slices of rustic bread.

Alphabetical Index

If you have any questions, suggestions or comments, please contact the Consumer Service of the Dr. Oetker Test Kitchen Telephone: + 49 800 71 72 73 74 Mon–Fri 8 am–6 pm, Sat 9 am–3 pm or the staff of Dr. Oetker Verlag Telephone: +49 521 52 06 51 Mon–Fri 9 am–3 pm.

Or you can write to us: Dr. Oetker Verlag KG, Am Bach 11, 33602 Bielefeld (Germany) or visit us on the Internet at www.oetker-verlag.de, www.facebook.com/Dr.OetkerVerlag or www.oetker.de.

Environmental notice — This book and its cover were printed on chlorine-free bleached paper. The shrinkwrapping to protect it from getting dirty is made from environmentally-friendly recyclable polyethylene plastic.

Editorial — Christina Langner

Cover photograph — Thomas Diercks (Fotostudio Diercks), Hamburg

Photographs in the book (recipes) — Fotostudio Diercks – Thomas Diercks/Kai Boxhammer/Christiane Krüger, Hamburg
also:
Walter Cimbal, Hamburg (pp. 10/11, 100, 147)
Janne Peters, Hamburg (pp. 52/53)
Antje Plewinski, Berlin (pp. 34, 152)

Small photographs in the book — Fotolia LLC, New York
also:
Torsten Elger, Berlin (p. 31)
Matthias Rübner, Forchheim (p. 72)
kontur:design, Bielefeld (p. 126)

Foreword, subheads and captions — Klaus Schäfer, Bonn

Food styling — Rocco Dressel, Hamburg

Recipe adviser — Olaf Brummel, Bielefeld

Translation — Rosetta Translations SARL, France

Graphic concept, design and cover design — kontur:design, Bielefeld

Reproduction — Repro Ludwig, Zell am See, Austria

Printing and binding — Druckerei Stürtz, Würzburg

ISBN: 978-3-7670-0657-7